Great Male Comedians

Other Books in the History Makers Series:

History MAKERS

Great Male Comedians

By Stuart A. Kallen

Lucent Books
P.O. Box 289011, San Diego, CA 92198-9011

Library of Congress Cataloging-in-Publication Data

Kallen, Stuart A., 1955–
    Great male comedians / by Stuart A. Kallen.
        p.   cm. — (History makers)
    Includes bibliographical references and index.
    ISBN 1-56006-739-X (alk. paper)
    1. Comedians—Biography—Juvenile literature. 2. Male comedians—
Biography—Juvenile literature. [1. Comedians.] I. Title. II. Series.
PN1583 .K28   2001
792.7'028'081—dc21   00-011971

Printed in the U.S.A.

CONTENTS

The literary form most often referred to as "multiple biography" was perfected in the first century A.D. by Plutarch, a perceptive and talented moralist and historian who hailed from the small town of Chaeronea in central Greece. His most famous work, *Parallel Lives*, consists of a long series of biographies of noteworthy ancient Greek and Roman statesmen and military leaders. Frequently, Plutarch compares a famous Greek to a famous Roman, pointing out similarities in personality and achievements. These expertly constructed and very readable tracts provided later historians and others, including playwrights like Shakespeare, with priceless information about prominent ancient personages and also inspired new generations of writers to tackle the multiple biography genre.

The Lucent History Makers series proudly carries on the venerable tradition handed down from Plutarch. Each volume in the series consists of a set of five to eight biographies of important and influential historical figures who were linked together by a common factor. In *Rulers of Ancient Rome*, for example, all the figures were generals, consuls, or emperors of either the Roman Republic or Empire; while the subjects of *Fighters Against American Slavery*, though they lived in different places and times, all shared the same goal, namely the eradication of human servitude. Mindful that politicians and military leaders are not (and never have been) the only people who shape the course of history, the editors of the series have also included representatives from a wide range of endeavors, including scientists, artists, writers, philosophers, religious leaders, and sports figures.

Each book is intended to give a range of figures—some well known, others less known; some who made a great impact on history, others who made only a small impact. For instance, by making Columbus's initial voyage possible, Spain's Queen Isabella I, featured in *Women Leaders of Nations*, helped to open up the New World to exploration and exploitation by the European powers. Unarguably, therefore, she made a major contribution to a series of events that had momentous consequences for the entire world. By contrast, Catherine II, the eighteenth-century Russian queen, and Golda Meir, the modern Israeli prime minister, did not play roles of global impact; however, their policies and actions significantly influenced the historical development of both their own countries and their regional neighbors. Regardless of their relative importance in the greater historical scheme, all of the figures chronicled in the History Makers series made contributions to posterity; and their public achievements, as well as what is known about their private lives, are presented and evaluated in light of the most recent scholarship.

In addition, each volume in the series is documented and substantiated by a wide array of primary and secondary source quotations. The primary source quotes enliven the text by presenting eyewitness views of the times and culture in which each history maker lived; while the secondary source quotes, taken from the works of respected modern scholars, offer expert elaboration and/or critical commentary. Each quote is footnoted, demonstrating to the reader exactly where biographers find their information. The footnotes also provide the reader with the means of conducting additional research. Finally, to further guide and illuminate readers, each volume in the series features photographs, two bibliographies, and a comprehensive index.

The History Makers series provides both students engaged in research and more casual readers with informative, enlightening, and entertaining overviews of individuals from a variety of circumstances, professions, and backgrounds. No doubt all of them, whether loved or hated, benevolent or cruel, constructive or destructive, will remain endlessly fascinating to each new generation seeking to identify the forces that shaped their world.

Laughing to Keep from Crying

Comedy is universal to all cultures and is as old as humanity itself. Archaeologists have found humorous drawings made twenty thousand years ago on caves in France. Around five thousand years ago, the Egyptian pyramids were marked with amusing graffiti by the slaves who were making fun of their slave masters. And in the fourth century B.C., Greek philosopher Aristotle said, "The gods too are fond of a joke."[1]

In modern times, comedic movies, TV shows, and CDs have become a multibillion-dollar business. The comedians featured in this book, Charlie Chaplin, Groucho Marx, Bill Cosby, Eddie Murphy, Jim Carrey, and Chris Rock, were *the* comedy innovators of their era and helped propel the comedy business to the pinnacle of popularity it has achieved today.

It has been said "laugh and the world laughs with you—cry and you cry alone," and these comedians have taken those words to heart, bringing people together by making them laugh. But the entertainment industry is an extremely difficult business in which to succeed, and though many comedians have made the world laugh, a common thread of tragedy and sorrow runs through their lives. To cite another cliché, they were often "laughing just to keep from crying."

Although they eventually became rich and famous, these big-name comedians have suffered great adversity. Chaplin, Cosby, Murphy, and Carrey lived through periods of dire poverty when they were children. Chaplin, Cosby, and Murphy lost one or both parents at an early age. Marx faced ongoing anti-Semitism, while Cosby, Murphy, and Rock had to contend with grinding racial prejudice. Along the way, some have had problems with their love lives, family relationships, or alcoholic parents.

Personal pain left these comedians feeling that they were on the outside of society looking in. And, ironically, they procured some of their best material from their greatest pain. Chaplin, who grew up in almost unimaginable poverty, is best known for his dirty, disheveled "Little Tramp" character, who is destitute but lovable. Cosby, whose father left his family when the comedian was very young, spent years talking about fatherhood and family bonds. And Chris Rock, who faced prejudice as the only black child in an all-white school, makes riotous observations about relations between the races.

Even after they had achieved success, many continued to suffer under the intense scrutiny of media and fans. Chaplin's failed love life was splashed across newspapers from coast to coast. Murphy and Carrey, among others, have had their less-than-successful movie projects scathingly analyzed and their personal missteps turned into tabloid magazine headlines.

Two traditional Greek theater masks portray the arts of comedy and tragedy. It is said that comedians are often "laughing just to keep from crying."

The urge to be clever, creative, and make people laugh, however, is inborn and hard to erase. Amazingly, the men featured here continued to produce immortal works even while sorrow occasionally gripped their personal lives. They continued to "give it up" for their fans, even as some of their fans turned their backs on them.

Laughter and tears—comedy and tragedy—have always been the two faces of theatrical entertainment, and these two opposites have always had a mutual relationship. For as long as people have felt fear or known pain, laughter has helped heal their souls. As such, it has been said that laughter is the best medicine. And if that is true then the comedy greats, from Chaplin to Rock, have acted as the doctors of comedy, providing soothing balm for psychic wounds in a sometimes less-than-happy world.

CHAPTER 1

Charlie Chaplin

Charlie Chaplin is one of the most famous comedians of all time. With characters such as the Little Tramp, Chaplin's movies made him one of the biggest stars of the 1910s and '20s, and continue to bring laughter and joy to people even today. Through his work, Chaplin found fame and fortune, but his childhood provided many more tears than laughs.

Charles Spencer Chaplin Jr. was born in the slums of South London, England, on April 16, 1889, the youngest of two children born to Charles and Hannah Chaplin. Charlie's boyhood home was in the Walworth district in a neighborhood dominated by rundown boarding houses, factories, and bleak landscapes. There were also many taverns, known as public houses or pubs, that served inexpensive food, beer, and liquor to the neighborhood's working poor. These pubs attracted customers by offering live comedy shows, singing, and dancing.

Charlie's parents were entertainers in this world of smoke-filled pubs. Hannah, using the stage name Lily Harley, played the role of a flirtatious maid in comedy skits, earning a small salary to support her family. Charlie later recalled his mother with great fondness in *Charles Chaplin: My Autobiography*:

> [Mother had a] fair complexion, violet-blue eyes and long light-brown hair that she could sit upon. [My brother] Sydney and I adored our mother. Though she was not an exceptional beauty, we thought her divine-looking. Those who knew her told me in later years that she was dainty and attractive and had compelling charm.[2]

Charlie's father was a talented singer and composer of sentimental ballads. He entertained in what was known as vaudeville theater—stage entertainment that featured singers, dancers, animal acts, jugglers, pantomimes, and comedians. One of the most popular features of vaudeville was slapstick comedy in which actors would throw pies, slap each other, break prop furniture, and play crude practical jokes on one another.

Charles Sr. was considered a star for a few years and earned top billing at several nationally famous vaudeville halls. His marriage with Hannah, however, was always difficult. As a traveling performer, Charles was often away from home, conducting romantic affairs with other women while on the road. Charles was also an alcoholic, and it was his love of drink that finally tore his marriage apart. The Chaplins separated in 1892 when Charlie was only three years old. He later recalled the circumstances of his father's life and death:

> It was difficult for vaudvillians not to drink in those days, for alcohol was sold in all theaters, and after a performer's act he was expected to go to the theater bar and drink with the customers. . . . [A] number of stars were paid large salaries not alone for their talent but because they spent most of their money at the theater bar. Thus many an artist was ruined by drink—my father was one of them. He died of alcoholic excess at the age of thirty-seven.[3]

Starring in many successful films during the 1910s and 1920s, Charlie Chaplin is one of the most famous comedians of all time.

Hard Times

After separating from her husband, Hannah found a new boyfriend, George Leo Dryden, with whom she had a child. After six months, however, Dryden took the child and disappeared forever. With no one to help her support her family, Hannah took work as a dressmaker and a nurse. She continued to sing in the theaters, but pay was meager and her children were forced to dress in rags and skip meals because of the lack of food.

By the time Charlie was five, his mother's voice, which was never strong, was made weaker with chronic laryngitis. As Chaplin wrote, "the slightest cold . . . lasted for weeks; but she was obliged to keep working, so that her voice grew progressively worse."[4]

One night Hannah appeared onstage before an audience of soldiers. As she tried to hit the high notes of a sentimental ballad, her voice cracked. The audience began to laugh, hiss, and yell rude comments. Hannah ran off the stage in tears, and the desperate owner of the music hall implored the five-year-old Charlie, who had been watching from the wings, onto the stage.

Hannah had taught her son to sing and dance, and the young boy now wracked his memory for a song to sing as he stood alone on center stage. Chaplin describes the scene:

> [Before] the glare of footlights and faces in smoke, I started to sing, accompanied by the orchestra, which fiddled about until it found my key. It was a well-known song called Jack Jones. . . .

Halfway through, a shower of money poured onto the stage. Immediately I stopped and announced that I would pick up the money first and sing afterward. This caused much laughter. The stage manager came on with a handkerchief and helped me to gatherer it up. I thought he was going to keep it. This thought was conveyed to the audience and increased their laughter, especially when he walked off with it with me anxiously following him. Not until he handed it to Mother did I return and continue to sing. I was quite at home. I talked to the audience, danced, and did several imitations.[5]

Hannah Chaplin's mental and physical health deteriorated as her family sank deeper into poverty.

Though her son was a success, Hannah never performed

13

again. The Chaplins were forced to move from the relative luxury of their three-room apartment into a series of attics and basements. After returning home from a hard day's work, Hannah's only joy in life came when her sons danced, sang, and did impersonations for her.

The Chaplins sank deeper into poverty, causing Hannah's physical and mental health to seriously deteriorate until she was finally forced to live in a hospital. In *Legendary Comedies*, Peter Guttmacher describes the next few years of Charlie's life:

> Charlie and his brother . . . were placed in a . . . workhouse called Lambeth until his mother's release [from the hospital]. The reunited family, which later moved to odoriferous lodgings between a slaughterhouse and a pickle factory, was so poor that the brothers shared one pair of shoes between them.[6]

The Lancashire Lads

Although they were reunited, Hannah's health never completely returned. When she was sick, the Chaplin boys temporarily moved into orphanages or stayed with their drunken father. There were periods of brief happiness each time Hannah was released from the hospital. In 1898, however, Charlie set off on his own when, with his father's encouragement, he took a job as an entertainer with a traveling vaudeville troupe known as the Eight Lancashire Lads.

The Lads traveled all over England, amusing audiences with dancing, impersonations, and comedy skits. Charlie toured with the group for two years, sometimes "bringing down the house" with his bawdy and hysterically funny animal imitations.

At the age of eleven, Charlie was reunited with his family when Hannah was released from yet another hospital. Their joy was tempered with sorrow, however. Charles Sr. died in 1901 at the age of thirty-seven from cirrhosis of the liver.

For the next several years, Charlie worked as a glass blower, messenger boy, printer, and physician's assistant. In 1903, Charlie came home one day from work and found that his mother's mental problems had become critical. Hannah's mental health had been deteriorating for some time and in her son's absence she had begun talking to invisible people while attempting to enter the homes of her neighbors. Chaplin, barely fourteen years old, recalled his feelings as his mother was taken to a mental institution: "I could feel only a numbing sadness. Yet I was relieved, for I knew that mother would be better off in the hospital than sitting alone in that dark room with nothing to eat. But that heartbreaking look as they led her [away] is one I shall never forget."[7]

The Mumming Birds

Charlie was once again on his own, but determined to find success in the entertainment business. Although he had nothing but rags to wear, he applied for work at one of London's most respected theatrical agencies. He was quickly hired to play the minor part of a page boy in a production of *Sherlock Holmes*, which toured England for forty weeks. The play was an immediate success, playing to kings, queens, princes, and princesses during its prestigious London run. Meanwhile Charlie fell in love with Marie Doro, one of the actresses in the play. Although little was spoken between them, Chaplin wrote, "I began to sink . . . into the hopeless mire of silent love."[8]

After the production ended, the teenage Chaplin spent the money he had put aside on alcohol and women, trying to forget his unfulfilled love for Doro. Chaplin was unemployed and heartbroken, and to make matters worse his mother's mental health had deteriorated to the point where she spent her days singing, crying, laughing, and dancing to music that only she could hear.

Fortunately Chaplin's theatrical career did not remain stagnant for long. Sydney, who was now twenty years old, was also an actor, and he helped his brother get roles in several moderately successful London productions. In 1908, Sydney landed Charlie a role with a well-respected London theatrical troupe, the Mumming Birds, run by a man named Fred Karno who managed thirty other theatrical troupes in Europe and North America. Originally Karno thought that Charlie was too serious to be a great comedian. Those fears melted away during Charlie's debut in a play called *The Football Match*, in which the young man demonstrated his slapstick abilities on a stage decorated like a locker room. Chaplin describes his first moments on the stage:

> There was music! The curtain rose! . . . That was my cue. In an emotional chaos I went on. One either rises to an occasion or succumbs to it. The moment I walked onto the stage I was relieved—everything was clear. I entered with my back to the audience—an idea of my own. From the back I looked immaculate, dressed in a frock coat, top hat, cane and spats . . . then I turned, showing my [brightly painted] red nose. There was a laugh. That ingratiated me to the audience. I shrugged melodramatically, then

15

Because of his popularity with the Mumming Birds, Chaplin was disliked by his fellow performers and even by Fred Karno himself.

snapped my fingers and veered across the stage, tripping over a dumbbell. Then my cane became entangled with an upright punching bag, which rebounded and slapped me in the face. I swaggered and swung, hitting myself with my cane on the side of the head. The audience roared.[9]

By the third night the sixteen-year-old Chaplin received applause the moment he stepped onstage. He soon signed a contract with Karno that guaranteed him a steady salary for a year.

Although Chaplin was a hit with audiences, other members of the Mumming Birds were often jealous of the young man who was stealing the show. They treated Chaplin as a junior member of the troupe, and the comedian responded by not speaking to anyone.

Despite the audiences Chaplin was attracting, even Karno disliked him, saying, Chaplin "wasn't very likable . . . I've known him to go whole weeks without saying a word to anyone in the company. . . . On the whole he was dour and unsociable."[10]

Beginning in 1910, the Mumming Birds toured the United States periodically for several years. During these long tours, the troupe played three shows a day for twenty-three consecutive weeks. The Mumming Birds performed in dance halls and theaters from New York City to Butte, Montana, to San Francisco. These tours could be compared to those of modern rock stars, with excessive parties, alcohol, drugs such as opium, and prostitutes in almost every town.

Hollywood Calling

Although vaudeville theater was wildly popular—especially in small western towns—a new form of entertainment was attracting audiences in droves. Motion pictures had been improving in quality since they were first invented by Thomas Edison in 1894; by 1910 there were hundreds of opulent movie theaters in cities across the country.

Charlie Chaplin (center, with life ring), poses with members of the Mumming Birds as they travel to the United States.

In 1913, while touring with the Mumming Birds, Chaplin received a telegram from Mack Sennett, founder of the Keystone Film Company. Sennett offered Chaplin $150 a week—two times his current salary—to appear in short silent films, which were shot at a rate of one film every three days. Though Chaplin believed these silent films were a crude form of entertainment, he accepted the producer's offer.

Keystone made rough-and-tumble slapstick comedies where actors tripped, fell, and wrestled with everyday objects such as chairs, ladders, and even automobiles. Inevitably, any character in the films who acted too haughty would receive a custard pie in the face. The films were often shot without scripts, and Sennett described his spontaneous production methods: "We have no scenario—we get an idea, then follow the natural sequence of events until it leads up to a chase, which is the essence of our comedy."[11]

Despite Chaplin's misgivings, he assumed the role of comedic movie star with ease. According to Guttmacher,

> In his screen debut, *Making a Living* (1913), Chaplin gleefully threw himself into the knockabout scenes, kicking, falling, and flailing with the best of them. . . . In *Mabel's Married Life* (1914), Chaplin was already giving an early glimpse of just how funny seriousness could be. In one of the most hilarious scenes of the movie . . . he has a lengthy, nuanced, volatile, and completely believable drunken discussion with a tailor's dummy.[12]

Chaplin debuted in his first full-length feature film, *Tillie's Punctured Romance*, in 1914. By this time millions of Americans were familiar with his battered bowler hat, undersized coat, oversized shoes, long baggy pants, bamboo cane, and "toothbrush" mustache made from a piece of black crepe paper glued under his nose.

By 1915, Chaplin was a huge star who had appeared in thirty-five silent films in a little over two years. Keystone, however, could no longer afford the star they had created. Chaplin left Sennett's company and took an offer from Chicago's Essanay Film Company. Essanay offered Chaplin a salary of $1,250 a week to make fourteen films in one year. At a time when a new car such as a Model T Ford cost $825, and a new house in Los Angeles cost under $3,000, this was an enormous salary.

With so much money at stake, Essanay officials began to wonder whether Chaplin was really all that popular. When they met the comedian at Chicago's Alexandria Hotel to sign the movie contract, they expressed their misgivings. According to Guttmacher,

As in a bit from one of his films, Chaplin's answer to their worries was to secretly engage a hotel messenger to walk around the lobby, loudly paging him. When the money men saw the huge crowd that gathered at the mere mention of Chaplin's name, they had no recourse but to sign on the dotted line.[13]

Actor, Producer, Director

Under contract at Essanay, Chaplin continued to refine his heartwarming tramp character in movie after movie. After he had made fourteen films for the company, however, the Little Tramp decided it was time to move on. Although Essanay offered Chaplin a $10,000 bonus for each picture, the comedian decided to sign with Mutual Film Corporation for $10,000 a week and a signing bonus of $150,000. At the age of twenty-six, Chaplin was the highest-paid actor in the movie business.

Mutual offered Chaplin complete artistic control over his movies, and the comedian seized the opportunity, producing twelve immortal films in the next eighteen months. As the most powerful man in show business, Chaplin exercised total control over every scene, telling each actor exactly how to move and what facial expression to use.

As a director, Chaplin worked without a script and shot each scene in order, often constructing an entire film from a single concept. Along the way the comedic genius wasted thousands of feet of film attempting to achieve perfection in every scene. In *The Immigrant*, for instance, Chaplin shot forty thousand feet of film; the final print contained only eighteen hundred feet.

A Wealthy Little Tramp

While his genius was apparent on-screen, Chaplin's solitary personal life had changed little in spite of his power and success. And despite the fact that he had grown up in dire poverty, he seemed to have little fascination with money. According to an article in *Harper's Weekly* published in 1916,

> [Chaplin's] only extravagance is a 12-cylinder automobile. He does not even allow himself the luxury of a wife. Jewelry, slow horses and fast company, country homes and *objects d'art* and other expensive fads of the predatory rich do not appeal to this slender young movie actor, who has risen in less than five years from obscurity to the distinction of being the highest-paid employee in the world.[14]

After signing with the Mutual Film Corporation, Chaplin held complete artistic control over all aspects of his movies.

Chaplin did use some of his money to help his mother Hannah, who had been living in a private hospital in London. The comedian bought her a small home by the ocean in California, where she lived happily for several years.

Although money may not have changed Chaplin very much, the big star faced new problems. According to Robyn Karney and Robin Cross in *The Life and Times of Charlie Chaplin,*

> On a trip to New York in February 1916 [Chaplin] had to leave his train at 125th Street station in order to avoid the huge crowd which had gathered to greet him at Grand Central. The Tramp was assuming a life of his own in Chaplin look-alike contests, comic strips, books, and a series of animated cartoons. Songs about Charlie . . . proliferated.[15]

Even though his popularity was rapidly growing, the comedian continued to feel like an outcast. He often wandered the streets of New York alone and dejected, embarrassed that he was too shy to make friends.

Around this time Chaplin met sixteen-year-old Mildred Harris, an extra in one of his films. Perhaps driven by his fear of loneliness, Chaplin married Harris after a short whirlwind courtship. Whatever his reasons for marriage, the comedian was not in love. According to Karney and Cross, "At the wedding, Chaplin was heard to remark that he felt sorry for [Mildred]."[16]

The couple later had a deformed child who lived only three days. Within months they were divorced. When the press found out about the failed marriage, rumors of infidelity and abuse appeared in headlines almost every day for a year.

Silent Films in a Talkie Era

Despite his personal problems, Chaplin continued to produce one movie after another. After his contract with Mutual expired in 1917, Chaplin signed a million-dollar contract with First National Exhibitors' Circuit. Then in 1919, hoping to exercise total control over the production and distribution of his films, Chaplin formed his own movie company, United Artists (UA), with actors Douglas Fairbanks and Mary Pickford and director D. W. Griffith. Unfortunately Chaplin's contract with First National prevented him from making any films with UA until 1923.

Pickford was one of the biggest stars of her day, and she and Chaplin became close friends. The two often wandered through the streets of Hollywood, discussing film ideas and the movie business. They were sometimes surrounded by hordes of admirers during these long walks. And since they were silent-film actors, according to Guttmacher, "no audience had ever heard them speak [so] the pair sometimes entertained themselves by talking in squeaky, high-pitched voices just to astonish their admirers."[17]

Unfortunately for Chaplin and other silent-film stars, technology was once again changing the film business. In 1927, the first "talkie," or film with sound, *The Jazz Singer*, became a box-office hit. Other talkies quickly followed, and the silent-film industry seemed doomed. Chaplin, however, refused to talk in any of his films until 1940, because he worried that his elegant English accent radically clashed with his image of a poor little tramp.

The comedian continued to face personal problems as well. In 1924 Chaplin had married Lita Grey, another sixteen-year-old actress. The couple had two children, Charles Spencer Chaplin III and Sidney Chaplin, who would both become actors. By the time of the first talkies, the couple had separated, and details of yet another Chaplin divorce were splashed across the pages of newspapers and magazines across the globe. Grey accused her husband of physical cruelties and sexual infidelities, which prompted newspaper columnists to call for a ban on Charlie Chaplin films. Meanwhile the government claimed that Chaplin owed $1 million in unpaid taxes, causing the comedian to suffer a nervous breakdown. While he was worried about losing his fortune and his film career, Chaplin's mother died in Glendale, California, on August 28, 1928.

Always a survivor, Charlie Chaplin continued to push on, writing, directing, and starring in some of the greatest silent films of all time—movies that were box-office hits even in an era of talkies.

Douglas Fairbanks and Mary Pickford helped Chaplin form a new movie company, United Artists.

In the 1931 film *City Lights*, the tramp falls in love with a beautiful blind girl and becomes her benefactor. The scene where he tries his hand as a prizefighter in order to win money for his love is still considered a comic masterpiece.

Chaplin's last silent film, *Modern Times*, depicts the Little Tramp as a victim of the machine age. He works on an assembly line and comically wrestles with a feeding machine. At the hands of his evil bosses, the tramp ends up in a mental hospital, and later a jail. His comedic misfortunes in this 1936 film proved to be a scathing political commentary during a time when factory workers were treated only as small cogs in a great machine.

The Great Dictator

In 1939, Chaplin decided to make his first talkie, *The Great Dictator*. In the film, Chaplin takes on no less a figure than the chancellor of Germany, Adolf Hitler. By this time, German armies were marching across Eastern Europe, conquering Czechoslovakia, Austria, and Poland. Although Hitler and his Nazi Party had become synonymous with evil, Chaplin could not help but notice that the German dictator looked a lot like the Little Tramp. When a friend sent him a postcard of Hitler making a speech, Chaplin wrote,

> The face was obscenely comic—a bad imitation of me, with its absurd mustache, unruly, stringy hair and disgusting, thin little mouth. I could not take Hitler seriously. . . . The [Nazi] salute with the hand thrown back over the shoulder, the palm upward, made me want to put a tray of dirty dishes on it. But when [Albert] Einstein [was] forced to leave Germany [because he was Jewish] the face of Hitler was no longer comic, but sinister.[18]

By the end of September 1939, England and France declared war on Germany and World War II had begun. In every country the Nazis invaded, they systematically rounded up Jewish people and either killed them immediately or sent them to forced labor camps, where most were executed or died from the effects of torture, starvation, or disease.

Horrified by these events, Chaplin set about making one of the most biting political satires in film history. Using sound for the first time, Chaplin mocked Hitler by changing his name to Adenoid Hynkel. To portray the character, Chaplin strutted about with his palm upraised, speaking in fake German gibberish.

Chaplin also plays the role of a Jewish barber. The comedian's third wife, actress Paulette Goddard, costars as the barber's wife.

23

In 1941, Chaplin released his first talkie, The Great Dictator, *a satire of German leader Adolf Hitler.*

In the film, Hynkel and the barber look very much alike, and their identities are inadvertently switched at the end of the movie, with the barber dressed like Hynkel making a plea for world peace: "We think too much and feel too little. More than machinery we need humanity. More than cleverness we need kindness and gentleness. Without these qualities life will be violent and all will be lost."[19]

When it was released in 1941, *The Great Dictator* was the most profitable film of the year, grossing $2 million and earning the New York Critics Award for Best Actor. Although some felt the film was in bad taste making light of such dark evil, Chaplin was the only director in Hollywood making anti-Nazi films at that time.

Meanwhile the stress of making *The Great Dictator* had caused Chaplin's marriage to Goddard to fall apart. The comedian soon married eighteen-year-old Oona O'Neill, daughter of American playwright Eugene O'Neill. This marriage proved to be a successful one, and the couple eventually had eight children.

Fade to Black

After World War II ended in 1945, former silent-film stars such as Charlie Chaplin were perceived as old-fashioned and out of touch. And political attitudes in the United States began to change as Americans feared that Communists from the Soviet Union were infiltrating their government. Many Hollywood stars were questioned before congressional committees for their liberal political activities during the depression before the war. Chaplin fell under suspicion for his social commentary and anti-big-business attitudes in films such as *Modern Times*.

The Federal Bureau of Investigation had been following Chaplin for years, keeping a large dossier on his sexual escapades and financial troubles. In the late 1940s, the U.S. attorney general opened an inquiry into Chaplin's "political nature and moral turpitude."[20] Upset with this turn of events, the comedian and his family moved to Switzerland. Then in 1952, the government charged Chaplin with being an "undesirable alien." Chaplin responded, saying, "I am not a Communist; neither have I ever joined any political party or organization in my life. I am what you call a peacemonger."[21]

In 1964, Chaplin published *My Autobiography,* providing rich insight into his life from the slums of London to his triumph as one of America's most respected film stars. In 1966 Chaplin made his last film, *A Countess from Hong Kong,* a comedy starring Marlon Brando and Sophia Loren.

By 1972, memories of the anti-Communist hysteria were long forgotten, and the Academy of Motion Picture Arts and Sciences wanted to present the eighty-two-year-old comedian with an honorary Oscar. Chaplin returned to America and created quite a stir among the press and public. He received a three-minute standing ovation at a gala reception at New York's Lincoln Center.

For the next five years it seemed as if the world wanted to make up for the pain Chaplin had suffered at the hands of the media and government. He was knighted by the queen of England and given awards at ceremonies throughout Europe.

Chaplin continued an active life with Oona by his side. Charlie Chaplin, the comic genius, peacefully died in his sleep on Christmas Day 1977, just a few months short of his eighty-ninth birthday.

CHAPTER 2

Groucho Marx

The Marx Brothers were the premier comedy team of the 1920s and '30s. Led by Julius "Groucho" Marx, their insane antics and trademark comedy bits left audiences gasping for breath as they laughed uncontrollably in movie theaters across the country. It must have been obvious to anyone who knew the Marx family in earlier years that the five sons born to Minnie and Simon Marx would someday be going into show business.

Minnie Marx was the guitar-playing daughter of Lafe Schoenberg, a ventriloquist and magician who had been an entertainer in Germany before he moved to the United States at the end of the nineteenth century. Minnie's mother was a yodeling harp player. Minnie's brother, Al, was a vaudeville singer and a comedian.

In 1884 Minnie married a man from eastern France, Simon "Frenchie" Marx. Between 1887 and 1901 the couple had five children, Leonard (1887), Adolf (1888), Julius (1890), Milton (1897), and Herbert (1901). Before long, these respectable names were abandoned, and each one of the Marx Brothers had a wacky nickname by the time the group was famous.

Leonard became Chico, because of his interest in girls, or "chicks." (His name was originally "Chicko" but the "k" was dropped in a graphic error in a handbill.) Adolf became known as Harpo for his beautiful harp playing, and Julius earned the nickname Groucho because of his grumpy demeanor. Milton was renamed Gummo for his gum-soled shoes. Herbert picked up the name Zeppo because he loved to do chin-ups, which made him look—at least to his brothers—like a performing monkey named "Zippo."

The five boys lived in an apartment in New York City with their parents, grandparents, a cousin, an aunt, and an uncle. Minnie sent Chico to piano lessons before he was thirteen, and he was instructed to teach Harpo what he had learned on the piano. Chico, however, was too busy hustling for money on the streets of New York, gambling in card games, and betting on horses. Harpo, who had dropped out of school in the second grade because a bully pushed him out of the second-story window of his classroom, was

Their insane antics made the Marx Brothers (left to right: Chico, Zeppo, Groucho, and Harpo) the most popular comedy group of the 1930s.

working as a bellboy, hot dog vendor, dog walker, and pin-setter at a nearby bowling alley. Instead of piano, he learned to play his grandmother's harp.

Groucho was the studious child who spent his time alone reading while the others were playing. When a doctor came to his family apartment to deliver Zeppo, Groucho decided he wanted to be a doctor. Fortunately for the world of comedy, those dreams were dashed when Groucho dropped out of school at the age of thirteen to help support his family.

Stranded in Cripple Creek

Freed from the rigors of schoolwork, Groucho began to earn a living as an entertainer. In his book *The Groucho Phile*, he describes his early foray in show business:

> The first real job I ever got was [at the amusement park] on Coney Island. I sang a song [while standing] on a beer keg and made a dollar. Later I sang in a Protestant church choir—until [they found out I was Jewish]. For that I got a dollar every Sunday. Before long I had to get a full-time job. . . . There wasn't enough money to feed the five brothers, parents, grandparents, [cousins, aunts, and uncles]. That's when I got into the big money, making $3.50 a week at the Hepner Wig Company. I lugged the big cans in which the wigs were washed. I'd been promised that someday, after I'd worked my way up, I'd be able to comb the wigs and put them on some famous actress's head.[22]

Although the wigs represented drudgery to Groucho, they were much more attractive to Harpo, who borrowed them for the comedy bits he began to perform.

At the age of fifteen Groucho answered a want ad for a boy singer in a vaudeville act that promised $4 a week plus room and board. When Groucho arrived for the audition he was greeted by Robin Larong, a man wearing lipstick and a silk kimono, posing as a woman. Larong hired Groucho and told him that they would be touring Grand Rapids, Michigan, and Denver, Colorado. Groucho explains how he prepared for the tour:

> We rehearsed about two weeks. Since the boss, Larong, lived in one room of this tenement [apartment], we did our rehearsing on the roof. In the August sun, the tin roof under our feet felt like a red-hot stove, but we were young, enthusiastic and hungry, and for the theater, ready to endure anything.
>
> When I said goodbye, my mother cried a little, but the rest of the family seemed able to contain themselves without too much effort. As a parting gesture, just as I was leaving, the dog bit me.[23]

The tour proceeded uneventfully until the group reached Cripple Creek, Colorado, where Larong ran off with another man. Groucho had saved some money for emergencies, but it was stolen. The young man was left stranded in Cripple Creek, forced to take a job delivering groceries by horse-drawn wagon.

The comedian eventually made his way back to New York and landed a job as a singer in a vaudeville variety show. When that job ended he was hired by a dramatic troupe that toured the United States for eight weeks. Once again he was left stranded, this time in New Orleans, when his money was stolen. To earn money Groucho joined a traveling burlesque show, in which scantily clad women danced and told bawdy jokes.

Minnie Marx disapproved of such indecent entertainment and ordered Groucho back to New York. After he returned, Minnie helped her sons put together their own stage act. To make sure that they would not be abandoned in some strange town, Groucho's mother decided that she would manage the troupe.

With Minnie's help, Gummo, Harpo, and Groucho (along with a neighborhood boy named Lou Levy) became the Four Nightingales. The group toured the United States from 1907 to 1910. Groucho commented on the act's travel arrangements:

Stranded in Cripple Creek, Colorado (pictured), Groucho was forced to take a job delivering groceries until he was able to return to New York.

Because we were a kid act, we traveled at half fare, despite the fact that we were all around twenty. Minnie insisted we were thirteen. "That kid of yours is in the dining car smoking a cigar," the [train] conductor told her. "And another one is in the washroom shaving." Minnie shook her head sadly [saying], "They grow so fast."[24]

In 1910 the Marx family moved to Chicago, a city central to the small-time vaudeville circuit, where the Four Nightingales played. While working one night in the east Texas town of Nacogdoches, the singing act became a comedy act. According to Guttmacher,

The audience . . . was less than attentive, and when news of a runaway mule all but vacated the theater, the Marx brothers became exasperated enough to start sending up [making fun of] their own songs and hurling rapid-fire insults to the yokels in the audience. Lines such as "Nacogdoches is full of roaches" made the locals laugh and cheer. The boys had hit on something. A little later in Denison, Texas, performing for a teachers' convention, they spontaneously decided to do a professorial skit with a German-accented Groucho in a frock coat, glasses, and a painted mustache. . . . A wig-topped Harpo played a moronic bumpkin. . . . When they got back from touring Chico joined the pack as Leo . . . (picking up an Italian accent . . .) with Uncle Al Shean writing music and skits for the boys. Harpo had only three lines; the review of the act touted Harpo as a brilliant mime but complained that the magic was lost each time he opened his mouth. He never [spoke] onstage or onscreen again.[25]

On to Broadway

For the next several years, the Marx Brothers honed their comedy talents on vaudeville stages from coast to coast. Groucho's greasepaint mustache, ever-present cigar, and round glasses topped with bushy, black, wiggly eyebrows quickly became the trademark of the act. As he traipsed across American stages with his bent-kneed duck walk, the comedian never missed an opportunity to ridicule pompous, snooty, or rich people.

The madcap Marx Brothers humor drew standing-room-only crowds, and the comedy team set an entertainment business record by playing sixty consecutive weeks in top-rated New York vaudeville theaters. Groucho was also finding happiness in his personal life. In 1920, the thirty-year-old comedian married the nineteen-year-old Ruth Johnson, who had originally been hired as Zeppo's dancing partner. Within a year, the couple had their first child, Arthur Marx.

In 1921, the Marx Brothers put up $4,000 of their own money to produce a silent film in a vacant lot in New Jersey. Although the movie, *Humor Risk*, was not a success, one of the actors decided to help the Marx Brothers underwrite a musical revue. The show, called *I'll Say She Is!* was made up of twenty-four scenes, some new, some taken from old bits the team had used for years. The production was put together on a shoestring budget, using scenery left over from other plays. Groucho wrote about *I'll Say She Is!*

> The scenery didn't quite fit, and the score was probably the most undistinguished one that ever bruised the eardrums of [an] audience. The girls, like all chorus girls, looked pretty good. The rest of the cast was strictly amateur night. . . . What we *did* have, however, was something money couldn't buy. We had fifteen years of sure-fire comedy material, tried-and-true scenes that had been certified by vaudeville audiences from coast to coast.[26]

The show opened in Philadelphia in 1923, and toured for about a year. When it finally opened in New York City at the Casino Theatre on Broadway on May 19, 1924, it was an overnight sensation. A *New York Times* critic wrote, "Such shouts of merriment have not been heard in the Casino these many years." A reporter for the *Post* said, "The Marx Brothers have left your correspondent too limp with laughter to do more than gasp incoherently at the most."[27]

No one could have been happier than Minnie Marx. Never before had four brothers performed together in a successful Broadway show. (Gummo was not in the revue.) Unfortunately Minnie had to see the play in less than perfect health. Days earlier, Minnie had been standing on a chair while being fitted for a dress for the premiere. She fell and broke her leg, and on opening night she had to be carried into the theater on a stretcher. She smiled and waved to the crowd as she was propped up in the front row. Despite her circumstances, Minnie would not have missed the debut. As Groucho wrote, "This was the culmination of twenty years of scheming, starving, cajoling and scrambling . . . and a little thing like a broken leg was not going to rob her of that supreme moment."[28]

Successful Cocoanuts

The success of the Marx Brothers coincided with an era known as the Roaring '20s. Although alcoholic beverages had been outlawed

The Marx Brothers are shown in a scene from their popular Broadway show Cocoanuts.

nationwide by a constitutional amendment in 1919, an active network of smugglers called bootleggers supplied cheap liquor to illicit clubs known as speakeasies. Meanwhile, the stock market was rising daily on a flurry of wild speculation, and many people—including Groucho—were making huge sums of money buying and selling often-worthless land in Florida.

The Marx Brothers produced their next Broadway show, *Cocoanuts*, based on these current events. *Cocoanuts*, written by George Kaufman and Morris Ryskind with music by famed composer Irving Berlin, was about the brothers' foibles while speculating on land in Florida. The show was a huge hit, playing 377 consecutive performances on Broadway. The following year, the show toured dozens of cities across America.

The Funny Family Man

With his newfound success Groucho bought a large home in Great Neck on Long Island, New York. He also tried to join a fancy beach club known as the Sands Point Bath and Sun Club. During the 1920s, however, there was open discrimination against Jewish people, and Groucho's application was refused by the club. Ever the comedian, Groucho simply made jokes in the face of this anti-Semitism. Groucho's son Arthur wrote about it in *My Life with Groucho*:

> [Groucho] filled out an application and handed it to the manager.
>
> "Are you Jewish?" asked the manager, not at all impressed that the applicant was a celebrity enjoying huge success on Broadway.
>
> "Not a practicing one," replied Groucho. "Actually I'm an American."
>
> "Well, we're very sorry, Mr. Marx," said the manager, "but we don't allow Jews to swim at our beach."
>
> "What about my son?" retorted Groucho. "He's only half-Jewish. Would it be all right if he went into the water up to his knees?"[29]

Shrugging off the rejection, Groucho instead took his business to the Lakeville Country Club, where he paid $5,000 to swim and play golf with famous stars of the day such as Eddie Cantor, Al Jolson, and Ruby Keeler. The club dues represented a huge sum of money, equal to the price of a large house in the upscale Hamptons located nearby.

Although his family enjoyed the country club, Groucho had little time for idle pleasures. *Cocoanuts* was playing six nights a week at 8:30 P.M. along with afternoon matinees on Wednesdays and Saturdays. Between shows Groucho could be seen dining at New York's most famous restaurants with celebrities such as boxer Jack Dempsey, screen siren Mae West, and the cowboy humorist Will Rogers. Sundays were the only nights the comedian spent at home.

Meanwhile, Chico, Harpo, and Zeppo had become heavy gamblers, wagering $2,000 to $3,000 on everything from horse races to softball games. Unlike his brothers, Groucho had little interest in gambling. Instead, as Arthur Marx recalled in 1985, he "was a family man . . . whose main interests were his children, his work, his books, his guitar and a large coterie of close friends."[30]

"Hello I Must Be Going"

After the success of *Cocoanuts*, nothing could stop the entertainment dynamo that was the Marx Brothers. Kaufman and Ryskind were asked to write another show for the comedy team. The result was *Animal Crackers*.

Animal Crackers is set in a Long Island mansion where a wealthy dowager is having a party. As is typical of Marx Brothers productions, the plot is simply an excuse for endless puns, twisted comedic logic, and ongoing ridicule of sophisticated, high-society manners. Groucho plays the part of a jungle explorer who tickles audiences with such lines as "One morning [in Africa] I shot an elephant in my pyjamas. How he got in my pyjamas I don't know."[31]

As in other Marx Brothers productions, Chico and Groucho wrestle physically and verbally while Harpo chases women, steals silverware, and—without saying a word—humorously confuses even the most basic logic. Several of the lines from the show, such as "Hello I must be going,"[32] are still quoted today.

Animal Crackers was the biggest Marx Brothers hit to date. The show was the hottest ticket in town, and even New York's biggest celebrities were turned away from the sold-out shows.

While the accolades—and money—rolled in, Groucho was working harder than ever. Paramount Pictures had signed the brothers to make a movie of *Cocoanuts*. This film was one of the

Pictured are Groucho and Zeppo (right) in Animal Crackers, *one of the Marx Brothers' biggest hits.*

first talkies, and Paramount set up a studio on Astoria, Long Island, so that the brothers could make the movie while still appearing on Broadway six nights a week. Arthur describes the hardship this caused for his father:

> Groucho would leave for the studio early in the morning, shoot until six or seven in the evening, and after a hasty meal with his brothers would go straight to the theater. It was hard work, for picture-making then was even more arduous than it is now. . . .

> The equipment was crude and constantly breaking down in the middle of the scene. Simple scenes had to be shot over as many as twenty and thirty times. The slightest noise two blocks away can ruin a take.

> "Sometimes I'd get so punchy," [Groucho said,] "that I find myself spouting the dialogue from *Animal Crackers* in a scene that I was doing in *Cocoanuts* and vice versa."[33]

To no one's surprise, *Cocoanuts* became box-office gold at movie theaters across the country. Money was pouring in, and family life seemed perfect with the birth of Marion Marx in 1928. Groucho was very conservative with his money and invested it in a place where he thought it would be safe—the stock market.

When the stock market crashed in October 1929, Groucho lost his entire fortune of $250,000—a sum equal to several million dollars today. As stockbrokers and investors committed suicide by jumping out of their office windows, Groucho went into a state of severe depression.

The fact that he was earning $2,000 a week in *Animal Crackers*, and the Marx Brothers had just signed a contract with Paramount for four more pictures at $200,000 each, was little consolation for the comedian. Although he still had this money coming in, the loss of his lifetime earnings affected his performances. He said, "I just didn't feel like making people laugh. I wanted to cry."[34]

Groucho had other reasons to be sad. His mother, Minnie, who had helped her sons achieve the pinnacle of show business success, died in 1929 at the age of sixty-four.

"You'll Duck Soup the Rest of Your Life"

The stock market crash in which Groucho lost his fortune was the beginning of the Great Depression. Theaters were empty as tens of thousands of people lost their jobs. It seemed, however, that unemployed and poverty-stricken Americans needed a good laugh more than ever. When the second Marx Brothers movie, a film adaptation of *Animal Crackers*, was released in August 1930, it garnered rave reviews and attracted huge crowds.

By 1931, however, the streets of New York City were filled with grim-faced men in soup lines and poverty-stricken women selling apples for pennies on street corners. For Groucho Marx it was time to trade the depressing streets for the golden sunshine of Hollywood. Groucho took to calling live theater the "Great Invalid," and wrote, "By switching to films, the Marx Brothers, in very short order, were better than ever and better off than ever."[35]

The Marx Brothers began making a movie a year. *Monkey Business* was released in 1931, *Horse Feathers* in 1932, and the hilarious *Duck Soup* in 1933. With the money earned from these movies, Groucho bought a fourteen-room mansion in Beverly Hills.

Duck Soup had all the classic ingredients of Marx Brothers madness. Set in the phony country of Freedonia and filmed shortly after Nazi dictator Adolf Hitler's rise to power in Germany, the film was, according to Guttmacher, "[heated] with nonstop gags [that] ridiculed everything military and pompously diplomatic . . . [dishing up laughs at] the expense of foreign tyrants."[36] The film struck such a critical note that Italian dictator Benito Mussolini banned *Duck Soup* in his country.

As for the film's title, Groucho famously explained, "Take two turkeys, one goose, four cabbages, but no duck, and mix them together. After one taste, you'll duck soup the rest of your life."[37]

For almost another decade the Marx Brothers continued their success with riotous movies such as *A Night at the Opera* and *A Day at the Races*. The money rolled in and the public was satisfied, but Groucho was frustrated by the business of making movies. It was very difficult to find writers in Hollywood who could write quick-witted, fast-paced dialogue that measured up to Groucho's comic genius. As a result, Groucho often found himself arguing with producers and directors who were interested only in cashing their checks after getting a hastily produced film into the theaters.

Endings and New Beginnings

By 1940, World War II had broken out in Europe, and the depression-era slapstick of the Marx Brothers was wearing thin as the public mood grew somber. In 1941, the Marx Brothers made *The Big Store*, announcing that it was their last movie together. Early in 1942 the comedy team that had made the world laugh for more than thirty years announced that it was breaking up.

Groucho's professional turmoil had bled over into his personal life as well. Groucho and Ruth had grown apart, she being a sensitive, shy person, and he being a wild nonconformist. In 1942 the couple separated.

Although the Marx Brothers were finished as a team, Groucho, who had always been the most popular member of the troupe, was not. Throughout the war he entertained soldiers, appearing at training camps and hospitals across America. He also hosted a thirty-minute radio variety show.

After he recovered from his divorce, Groucho began dating. In 1945 the fifty-five-year-old comedian married the twenty-four-year-old Kay Gorcey, an aspiring singer and dancer. Within a year the couple had a child, Melinda, and in 1947 Groucho became a grandfather, with the birth of his son Arthur's first child.

After Melinda was born, the Marx Brothers reunited for another movie called *A Night in Casablanca*. Although Groucho's fans were glad to see him on the big screen again, the comedian was less than thrilled with the project. Groucho wrote, "Chico, Harpo and I probably wouldn't have teamed up again if Chico hadn't needed the money. I was about to begin raising a second family, and, at my age, that was a full-time occupation."[38]

Duck Soup provided audiences with nonstop laughs at the expense of the era's military tyrants.

You Bet Your Life

In 1947, Groucho appeared in film for the first time without his brothers in *Copacabana*. That same year the comedian began hosting a radio quiz show called *You Bet Your Life*. This was a step down careerwise for a box-office smash like Groucho, but he said, "Maybe I thought I was slumming, but I needed the work."[39]

The format of *You Bet Your Life* consisted of average Americans trying to win large sums of money by answering trivia questions posed by the wisecracking Groucho. The show started out with very low ratings, but soon became a hit. Yet as the ratings climbed, Groucho's personal life once again sank into confusion. After only three years of marriage Groucho and Kay were divorced, with Groucho retaining custody of Melinda. By 1949, however, Groucho was a certified radio star.

Meanwhile the Marx Brothers appeared in a film called *Love Happy*, in which Groucho got to dance with the budding star Marilyn Monroe. Critics panned the film, which was the last movie that the Marx Brothers made together.

Around this time the first television sets were sold to the general public. Groucho suddenly found himself in demand for this rapidly developing new medium, and in 1950 *You Bet Your Life* debuted on the NBC television network. Although the entertainment business was changing around him, Groucho felt little need to change his style. As he wrote before the show's first season, "I'm going to keep my cigar, my leer and any old ad lib wisecracks I find lying around. The mustache is my own now. I bought it from the upstairs maid."[40]

"The Same Old Groucho"

You Bet Your Life ran for eleven years. In 1952 the sixty-four-year-old comedian married the twenty-year-old Eden Hartford. Groucho continued to appear in movies throughout the '50s, and *You Bet Your Life* remained on the air until 1961. That same year, Chico, seventy-four, became the first Marx Brother to die. Harpo died at the age of seventy-five in 1964.

Groucho's marriage to his third wife ended in 1969, and the comedian suffered a series of heart attacks and strokes in the early 1970s. By this time, many in the entertainment business were eager to honor the comedian for the lifetime of joy he had provided for his fans. In 1972, Groucho was honored in France at the Cannes Film Festival, where he was presented with the French government's *Commandeur des Arts et Lettres*, a highly respected award.

In his later years, Groucho used his wisecracks to entertain both audiences and contestants as the host of You Bet Your Life.

By 1975 the eighty-five-year-old Groucho was spending more and more time in bed. His health continued to deteriorate, until the great comedian died on August 19, 1977. After Groucho's death, Arthur found a note among his father's personal items. In it, Groucho said he wanted to be buried at the Westwood Cemetery next to the body of Marilyn Monroe. Arthur wrote, "The same old Groucho. Even after he had shuffled off his mortal coil, he wanted to lie throughout eternity alongside the most glamorous sex symbol of the age."[41] Although Groucho's final request was never realized, he will long be remembered as one of the funniest comedians who ever graced stage or screen.

CHAPTER 3

Bill Cosby

Comedians such as Groucho Marx were already part of a bygone era when Marx's show *You Bet Your Life* went off the air in the early 1960s. By this time American comedy had become edgier and its social statements bolder. Bill Cosby came along during this time of social change, and when he first found fame he was considered one of the trendiest comics of his day.

Although he would eventually be one of the richest entertainers in history, Cosby was born into a world of poverty and racism. William Henry Cosby Jr. was born on July 12, 1937, the first child of Anna and William Henry Cosby Sr. The Cosby family lived in the African American neighborhood of Philadelphia named Germantown but called "the Jungle" by local residents. During this era, discrimination against African Americans was common, and most black people held low-paying jobs, living in segregated neighborhoods where widespread poverty was the fact of life.

Bill's father had a relatively good job as a welder, and the Cosbys lived in modest but decent apartments. After Bill was born, however, the Cosbys had three more sons in several years, and William Sr. began to drink heavily. As more of their father's wages went to alcohol, the family was forced to move into shabbier apartments in poorer neighborhoods. As Bill later said, "My father is an intelligent man who failed in life. . . . When I was a child, we kept moving down the economic ladder."[42]

The Cosbys ended up living in the housing projects known as the Richard Allen Homes. When Bill's younger brother James died of rheumatic fever at the age of six, William Sr. abandoned his family and joined the navy. As the oldest son, the eleven-year-old Bill became the man of the household. William Sr. sent money home occasionally but Anna was forced to work up to twelve hours a day as a cleaning woman. Bill added to the household income by shining shoes before going to school in the morning. After school, he came home and took care of his brothers until his mother's long workday had ended. During the summers he worked at local grocery stores for $8 a week.

Bill Cosby is pictured onstage during one of his many sold-out live performances.

Growing Up Funny

In spite of the hardships he faced, Cosby was known as the class clown at school. Unfortunately his teachers did not always appreciate his humor. Mary Forchic, Bill's sixth-grade teacher, was particularly annoyed by the young comedian's constant joking. According to biographer Ronald L. Smith, the teacher once scolded Bill with this prophetic admonition: "In this classroom, there is one comedian and it is I. If you want to be one, grow up, get your own stage, and get paid for it."[43]

Although Cosby's antics may have irritated his teacher, Forchic also encouraged the young man, writing on his report card, "He would rather be a clown than a student and feels that it is his mission to amuse his classmates in and out of school . . . [but] he should grow up to do great things."[44] Forchic channeled Cosby's talents by casting him in several school plays. His first public performance was as the star of a production titled *King Koko from Kookoo Island.*

As class clown, Cosby was a popular student, but this flair did little to enhance his scholastic pursuits. Though Cosby managed to advance to the next grade each year, his report cards showed mostly Cs and Ds. The young man did, however, score near the top of his class on IQ, or intelligence quotient, tests. As a result, he was sent to a special all-boys school for gifted students called Central High School.

Cosby quickly realized he was out of his league among the rich and intelligent students at Central. As Smith writes,

> Cosby was stifled by the atmosphere at the school, where "gifted" meant cliques of smug, self-assured, and disdainful kids. Cos was out of his depth and the only thing he could do was demonstrate class-clown bravado, showing the miniature whiz kids the difference between uptight and cool.
>
> Cos would be sitting in class, swapping the textbook for a comic book. The teacher would come over, take it, and utter an archly meaningful "You'll get this back at the end of the school year."
>
> And Cos would say, "Why? Does it take that long to read it?"[45]

Such attitude did little to endear him to his teachers. After his sophomore year Cosby was transferred back to his old neighborhood school, Germantown High, where he was made captain of both the football and track teams. His learning abilities did not improve, however, and still in high school at the age of nineteen, Cosby dropped out. Following in the footsteps of his father, the young man joined the navy. In the service, Cosby trained to become a physical therapist.

Jokes from a Tabletop

As a physical therapist Cosby helped wounded veterans learn to walk and feed themselves again. He also made them laugh, thereby helping them relieve some of the pain they were experiencing. During his four-year stint in the navy, Cosby came to realize the importance of education. He later stated, "I met a lot of guys in the navy . . . who didn't have as much 'upstairs' as I knew I did, yet they were struggling away for an education. I finally realized I was committing a sin—a mental sin [by not utilizing my intelligence]."[46]

Cosby won several track and field awards in the navy, and later used them to get an athletic scholarship at Temple University. At age twenty-three he became a promising track star at Temple, running, throwing discus and javelin, and jumping hurdles. He also became right halfback on the varsity football team. After only one game, however, Cosby broke a collarbone and spent the rest of his football career as a second-stringer.

To finance his education, Cosby took a job for $5 a week as a bartender in a cramped cellar club called the Underground. Realizing that he could make larger tips by making the customers laugh, the young man offered humorous dialogue along with the drinks he served. According to Smith, "Cosby . . . earned tips as the funniest, most charming bartender the place had ever seen. He wrote down jokes he heard on TV, gags he picked up from the comedy records students were beginning to play."[47]

The owner of the bar appreciated Cosby's wit and asked him to tell jokes to the customers at their tables. Word of the young man's quick wit spread throughout the community, and people soon began crowding into the Underground to hear Cosby's act. The club's owner took advantage of the situation by moving his funny bartender into a slightly larger club in the same building called the Cellar. The Cellar did not have a stage so the fledgling comedian performed while sitting in a chair placed on top of a table.

The Burlesque Circuit

Flush with success, the tabletop comic began to study the jokes, rhythm, and delivery of the era's well-known comedians such as Mort Sahl, Jonathan Winters, and Shelly Berman. He also started to incorporate his own personal experiences into his comedy routines, joking about school, the navy, and his less-than-stellar career with the Temple University football team.

As a college student, Bill Cosby was a member of the Temple University football team.

Cosby had entered the comedy business at a good time. In 1959, Shelly Berman had become the first comedian to see his comedy record "go gold," or sell more than 500,000 copies. The next year, social satirist Mort Sahl was featured on the cover of *Time* magazine. Comedy was fast becoming a booming business and record producers were signing dozens of unknown comics to make albums. As Smith writes, "The 'new wave' of stand-up comics was making more money in a season than any football player, college professor, or even the president of the United States."[48]

Cosby continued to take classes at Temple and participate in the track meets. But it was obvious that his comic talents far surpassed his interest in academics or sports—and the extra money he earned helped pay for his living expenses. However, there were few comedy clubs in Philadelphia in the early 1960s, and most of Cosby's early gigs consisted of telling jokes at seedy burlesque theaters between performances by strippers. Obviously this was not an optimum showcase for a young, black comedian.

In addition to studying the top comedians of the day, Cosby began to incorporate personal experiences into his routine.

Cosby often clashed with the theater managers who wanted him to "work blue," that is, tell dirty jokes and shock the patrons by swearing. Other club owners wanted Cosby to tell racial jokes, which were popular because the civil rights movement was making gains in the United States. Cosby, however, drew on his childhood experiences—his mother, family, and friends—as a source for his humor. As a result, the young comedian was fired from many of his first jobs away from the Cellar.

By 1962, Cosby realized that he would never become famous playing the Philadelphia burlesque circuit. Scraping together his last few dollars, he bought a train ticket to New York City, where beatniks and avant-garde artists were at the center of a hip, new social scene in Greenwich Village. After a few auditions, Cosby's talents were recognized, and he was hired to work at the Gaslight, the premier coffee house in the Village.

New York, New York

Cosby was ecstatic when he was told he would be paid what seemed like the large sum of $60 a week at the Gaslight. His heart sank, however, when he realized that he had nowhere to stay in New York. Unable to afford the city's expensive hotel rates, the comedian took up residence on a cot in an upstairs storeroom at the Gaslight. He was also forced to skip meals in order to save money, sometimes getting by on one small meal per day.

Professionally, Cosby faced tough competition, sharing stages with young comedians such as Woody Allen, Mel Brooks, Joan Rivers, Lenny Bruce, and others who would go on to become very famous. But the young comic from Philadelphia had a different style that attracted rapt attention. As Smith writes,

> What impressed fellow comics was Cosby, not his material. The key to the success of a comic is the personality. . . . [There] is a difference between saying funny things and saying things funny.
>
> Cosby said things funny. And he was cool. . . . While other comics fretted, [and were] nervous wrecks, rushing their lines and showing the audience their fear, Cosby took his time. When things were going badly, he could even make a joke of it. One night when the new gags weren't working . . . Cos simply curled up out of harm's way and did his show from under a piano.[49]

After one successful winter at the Gaslight, Cosby was signed by a manager named Roy Silver, who got Cosby's salary increased to

$175 a week, a huge sum at the time. Meanwhile a glowing review in the *New York Times* in the summer of 1962 brought swarms of fans to the Gaslight, and Silver used the publicity to book the comedian in Chicago, Washington, D.C., and other big cities.

Hit Records, Love, and Marriage

Cosby's comedy career was increasingly interfering with the demands of college. Although it was a bitter disappointment to his mother, the comedian finally dropped out of school to pursue his comedy career full-time. By this time he was pulling in $500 a week during an era when a worker earning minimum wage was paid $50 a week.

By 1964, Cosby was in great demand at clubs across the country, and he even got a chance to appear on TV on *The Tonight Show*, the pinnacle of exposure for up-and-coming comedians. After his successful television appearance, the comedian released his first comedy album called *Bill Cosby Is a Very Funny Fellow . . . Right!*, which was recorded live at a nightclub called the Bitter End in Greenwich Village. The album sold well and was nominated for a Grammy for the Best Comedy Album in 1963.

Cosby didn't win the Grammy that year, but his disappointment was softened by his newfound love. While playing a show in Washington, D.C., the comedian met a nineteen-year-old psychology major named Camille Hanks who attended the University of Maryland. After a whirlwind romance—and over the strenuous objections of her well-to-do parents—the couple married on January 25, 1964. Their honeymoon was in no way traditional. The couple spent several weeks traveling between San Francisco, Los Angeles, and Lake Tahoe, California, where Cosby performed nightly.

Meanwhile, the comedian continued to find success in the record business. His second album, *I Started Out as a Child*, and his third album, *Why Is There Air?*, both won Grammy awards.

Breaking Barriers on TV

By now Cosby's offbeat brand of comedy was familiar to those in the entertainment business. Sheldon Leonard, the producer behind successful situation comedies such as *The Andy Griffith Show* and *The Dick Van Dyke Show*, felt that Cosby would be perfect for a new spy series he was developing called *I Spy*. Leonard wanted Cosby to play the role of Alexander Scott, a tennis trainer whose client, played by Robert Culp, was an international tennis star whose world travels covered for his real job as a spy.

At the time there were very few African Americans on television, and none costarred equally with a white man. The executives who ran the network feared that racist station owners in the South would refuse to run *I Spy* and the sponsors would be afraid to advertise.

The show faced other problems as well: Cosby's easygoing wit on the comedy stage did not transfer well to a serious role. As an actor, Cosby was stiff and often had trouble delivering his lines to the camera. As Adler explains,

> Cosby was warm, smiling, and charismatic in his own milieu of comedy, but he couldn't play a straight role! He kept reading his lines as if he were alone in front of a camera. Instead of reacting, he was simply reading lines to himself.

Despite her parents' objections, Bill Cosby married Camille Hanks on January 25, 1964.

Luckily Cosby was a natural actor and fast study. With the help of Culp, an old pro, and Leonard, Cosby finally got the hang of doing straight acting.[50]

When it premiered in 1965, *I Spy* was an instant success. The twenty-seven-year-old Cosby was elevated into a national star overnight. In addition, Cosby's role on the show helped change the racist manner in which blacks were portrayed on television. As *Newsweek* magazine wrote, "[Cosby] has completely refurbished the television image of the Negro. He is not the stereotyped, white-toothed Negro boy with a sense of good rhythm. He is a human being, and a funnier, hipper human being than anyone around him."[51]

Cosby was now making more than $2 million annually, a mere five years after he had launched his comedy career. Some club dates paid as much as $50,000 a week, and Cosby continued to release one comedy album per year, earning four Grammys between 1966 and 1969. To add to this happiness, the Cosbys had their first child, Erika, on April 8, 1965. Their second daughter, Erinn, was born about a year later, and a third child, a son named Ennis, was born in 1969.

College, Cartoons, and Movies

When *I Spy* was canceled in 1969, Cosby was given the go-ahead to star in his own television show. For a theme, Cosby drew on his early desire to coach sports at an inner-city school. As such, his new program, *The Bill Cosby Show*, was about Chet Kinkaid, a gym teacher in a poor Los Angeles neighborhood. Although the show was funny and engaging, it aired opposite *The Ed Sullivan Show*, which featured acts such as the Beatles and was extremely popular. *The Bill Cosby Show* started out strong, but its ratings fell, and it was canceled after only two seasons.

After *The Bill Cosby Show* went off the air, the comedian shocked his colleagues by leaving Hollywood to return to college. When Cosby began attending classes at the University of Massachusetts in Amherst in 1971, it had been almost a decade since he had dropped out of Temple University. While earning a master's degree in education, the comedian commuted to New York City and Los Angeles to produce a Saturday morning cartoon designed to help educate children.

In September 1972 *Fat Albert and the Cosby Kids* premiered on CBS. Each episode taught a moral lesson and made kids laugh. While attending school and working on his cartoon series, Cosby

Cosby (pictured with costar Robert Culp) helped change the way blacks were portrayed on television with his role in the hit TV show I Spy.

also appeared on an educational show on the Public Broadcasting System (PBS) called *The Electric Company*.

Two shows and a college classroom, however, were not enough for the hardworking Cosby. The comedian continued to appear in nightclubs across the country and record comedy albums, and he even tried his hand at singing on a 1974 album called *At Last Bill Cosby Really Sings*. Cosby also put together a variety show on CBS called *The New Bill Cosby Show*. Unfortunately the show ran opposite the extremely popular *Monday Night Football* and went off the air after only one year.

During this era Cosby also moved onto the big screen, writing and producing a modestly popular film about an African American cowboy called *Man and Boy*. He also starred in a comedic detective movie called *Hickey and Boggs* with his former *I Spy* costar Robert Culp. This movie, however, was a financial disaster.

Cosby's luck on the big screen improved in 1974 when he costarred with respected African American actor Sidney Poitier in the hit *Uptown Saturday Night*, a film about two friends living in the Harlem neighborhood of New York City. Meanwhile the Cosby family continued to grow: A girl named Ensa Camille was born in April 1973, and a fifth child, another girl, Evin, was born in 1975.

Bad Reviews

In 1976, a beaming Bill Cosby was awarded a doctorate in education at the University of Massachusetts, officially making him Dr. William H. Cosby Jr. This degree would be a high point during the second half of the 1970s when Cosby's career went on to face cancellations, bad reviews, and some controversy.

His new show about a middle-class family, simply titled *Cos*, lasted a mere seven weeks on ABC. As the 1970s progressed, the comedian acted in several forgettable movies, including *Mother, Jugs, and Speed* with Raquel Welch and *A Piece of the Action* with James Earl Jones. These movies and several others starring Cosby received terrible reviews from critics and did poorly at the box office. Even the 1978 movie *California Suite*, written by award-winning playwright Neil Simon, was mercilessly panned by critics, who claimed that Cosby's slapstick behavior while trashing a hotel room in one scene denigrated African Americans.

Cosby did find success, however, acting in television commercials. The comedian's sincere manner was used in advertisements selling, among other products, Jell-O Pudding, White Owl Cigars, and Pan American Airlines. By becoming a commercial spokesman, Cosby once again drew the ire of critics. The *Village Voice* wrote, "Cosby has become unfunny in recent years, a monotonous young fogey capitalizing wherever he can on his splendiferous teacher thing. . . . He has evolved into a kind of self-parodying sap."[52]

Happiness with the Huxtables

At the beginning of the 1980s, Cosby continued to make large sums of money making commercials and appearing live in casinos in Lake Tahoe and Las Vegas. In 1983 he released a successful film, *Bill Cosby Himself*, that simply featured Cosby doing his stand-up routine alone onstage.

One night while watching cable television in Las Vegas, Cosby saw three different movies in a row that featured scenes of sex, violence, and drug use. Ignoring his previous failures, the comedian decided it was once again time to try his hand at a family-oriented television show. His plan for a sitcom about a loving African American family was rejected by the three major networks, however, for prime-time lineups during that period featured sexually oriented soap operas and violent detective shows.

Cosby forged on, teaming up with a production company to shoot a demonstration show, known as a pilot, about a doctor named Heathcliff Huxtable. Dr. Huxtable was married to a lawyer named Claire, and the couple had four children. Drawing from the comedy material he had been using for years, Cosby combined moral lessons with gentle humor. NBC liked the pilot and began airing *The Cosby Show* in September 1984.

At last Cosby found the formula to entertain the American television-viewing public. *The Cosby Show* became the third most-watched prime-time show in its first year. Not everyone loved the show, however, including some black critics who felt that Cosby's portrayal of an upper-middle-class African American

Despite criticism that it did not accurately portray the typical black family, The Cosby Show *was the number one show on television for five years.*

family did not address the real problems faced by blacks. Smith listed some of the questions posed to Cosby by critics:

> Aren't you out of touch? . . . Will you show the *real* black American family? What about social problems? What about white *versus* black? Isn't it a fairy tale to portray blacks as doctors and lawyers? How come you don't talk . . . real black dialect? And why aren't you having the family live in the ghetto?

> [Cosby responded by saying,] Why do they want to deny me the pleasure of being an American and just enjoying life? . . . Why must I make all the black social statements? Why not do a show [with class] . . . something to be proud of . . . to show that we have the same kinds of wants and needs as other American families?[53]

In the end, the public and the critics agreed with Cosby, and *The Cosby Show* was the number-one prime-time show for the following five seasons.

The success of the show made Bill Cosby one of the most famous and well-paid comedians in the United States. By portraying a black family as a group of average people who had achieved the American dream, Cosby once again helped change the negative ways that blacks were often shown on TV. The Huxtables broke the stereotypes, and also showed a family much like the Cosbys were in real life. The comedian's ex-manager Roy Silver explains, "[Bill Cosby] never drinks. He never did drugs. [He's] married to the same wife, has five kids, [is] well spoken, articulate, [and] sincere."[54]

Charitable Giving

After eight seasons, *The Cosby Show* finally went off the air on April 30, 1992. By this time, the comedian was consistently listed in *Forbes* magazine as one of the five highest-paid entertainers in the world. Cosby had become so rich, in fact, that in 1992, he attempted to buy the multibillion-dollar NBC television network. Although this deal never materialized, the comedian returned to TV that year as the host of *You Bet Your Life*, a remake of the quiz show made famous by Groucho Marx between 1950 and 1961.

In 1997, Bill Cosby faced the biggest tragedy of his life when his only son, Ennis, was murdered by a robber while stopped on a freeway ramp to change a flat tire on his car. Ennis had been the inspiration for Theo Huxtable, Cosby's fictional son on *The Cosby Show*. Through their grief the family used the murder of

Escorted by police officers, Cosby is shown leaving his New York City apartment shortly after his son Ennis was murdered on a California freeway.

their son to make the world a better place, setting up the Ennis William Cosby Foundation to grant scholarships and offer help to learning-impaired children.

Cosby has also contributed millions of dollars to other charitable funds throughout the years. In 1998, the comedian was honored by the highly respected John F. Kennedy Center for the Performing Arts in Washington, D.C. The center's website lists Cosby's accomplishments:

> Cosby's success on television has been matched in other areas. In 1986 he broke Radio City Music Hall's 53-year-old attendance record for his concert appearance. Cosby's also a giant in the publishing world. *Fatherhood* (1986) became the fastest-selling hardcover book of all time, remaining for more than half of its fifty-four weeks on *The New York Times* Best Seller List as Number 1. It has sold 2.6 million hardcover copies and 1.5 million paperbacks. *Time Flies* had the largest single first printing in publishing history—1.75 million. He has had 21 albums on the national pop charts (three in the Top 10 and three more in

the Top 20) which have earned him eight Gold Records and five Grammy Awards.

A crusader throughout his career for a better world, his great success in the world of entertainment is complemented by his involvement with a host of charity organizations, making substantial gifts in support of education, most notably to predominantly black colleges and to various social service and civil rights organizations.[55]

Though born to a poor family in Philadelphia, Cosby overcame discrimination and hardship to become one of the most successful comedians in history. He helped people see humor in everyday family life and focused on the positive in an often negative world. By laughing at his own foibles, Bill Cosby showed people that they can laugh at themselves and still maintain dignity and respect, two things that never seem to go out of style in an ever-changing world.

CHAPTER 4

Eddie Murphy

While Bill Cosby charted a long, steady career emphasizing the similarities between people, Eddie Murphy took a different road to comedy stardom. From the moment he burst on the scene on television's *Saturday Night Live* at the age of twenty, Murphy's routines have been meant to shock and amuse by pointing out the behavioral quirks of various groups.

Edward Regan Murphy was born on April 3, 1961, in Brooklyn, New York. Eddie was the youngest of two children born to Lillian and Charles Murphy. The Murphys lived in a small apartment in a housing project in the Bushwick section of Brooklyn. The neighborhood had its share of drug dealers, muggings, and murders, but the Murphys were not as poor as many of their neighbors. Lillian worked as a telephone operator and Charles as a New York City transit police officer. At night Murphy's father told jokes and worked as an emcee (master of ceremonies) at local nightclubs. As Murphy later told an interviewer, however, "My parents broke up when I was three. . . . After the divorce, [my dad] and I used to go out on weekends to movies, but I don't really have a clear memory of him."[56]

Eddie Murphy's style of comedy was meant to shock audiences while pointing out people's differences.

The Good and Bad of Life

The years after Murphy's father left were some of the worst in the young boy's life. Money was in short supply, and Murphy's mother worked long hours to support her family. At one point, she became seriously ill and was forced to spend an entire year in a hospital. Eddie and his brother Charles were sent to live in a foster home run by a woman he called "a black Nazi." The woman fed him strange food such as fried pigs' tails and whipped him when he would not eat it. As Murphy later recalled, "Those were *baaad* days. Staying with her was probably the reason I became a comedian."[57]

While an evil foster mother may have helped Murphy express himself as a comedian, the young man was always known for his sense of humor. As a child he watched cartoons for hours at a time, learning to imitate the voices of animated characters such as Bugs Bunny, Dudley Do-right, and Bullwinkle. He also cracked up his friends at school by imitating the principal and various teachers.

It was his humor that helped Murphy through tough times—especially in 1969 when Charles Sr. was stabbed to death by his girlfriend. Any hopes Murphy had of getting to know his father were dashed, and the comedian later said the death of his father was one of the greatest tragedies of his life.

Move to the Suburbs

Things improved for Murphy when his mother began dating Vernon Lynch, an amateur boxer and boxing instructor who worked in a Long Island ice cream factory. Lynch provided a strong father figure for the young man, and married Lillian when the boy was ten. Lynch moved his new family into a nice ranch house in the predominantly black, suburban Roosevelt neighborhood on Long Island. Murphy was sad to leave his childhood friends behind, but the big house in the middle-class suburb provided a welcome getaway from the hardships of inner-city life.

As for so many other suburban children, television was Murphy's constant companion. As biographer Frank Sanello writes, "Lillian recalled that her son would lock himself in his room for hours, with the hi-fi blaring Elvis [Presley], while he wrote comedy scripts. TV was his teacher in this bedroom-classroom."[58] Besides Presley, Murphy loved the karate movies of Bruce Lee and *West Side Story*, the classic 1960 musical about New York street gangs. Unlike most other boys his age, Murphy had an almost neurotic fear of pain and so avoided playing sports.

Although Murphy could do a dead-on imitation of Elvis Presley, or speak for hours like Bugs Bunny, he earned terrible grades at school. In order to avoid being kept back, he was forced to attend summer school every year from the eighth grade until he graduated. Lillian often worried that her son would not be able to attend college and would face a life of minimum-wage poverty.

Murphy had other plans for his life, however. While his friends were reading their schoolbooks and shooting hoops, Murphy spent his after-school hours in the basement studying the comedy records of comedians such as Bill Cosby and Richard Pryor. He also dressed up as Elvis and played the singer's *Live from Madison Square Garden* album while lip-synching in front of a mirror.

Fifteen-Year-Old Headliner

On July 9, 1976, when he was in tenth grade, Murphy got a chance to demonstrate his talents to an audience when he was asked to host a talent show at the Roosevelt Youth Center. As emcee, the young man told jokes between acts and lip-synched to a record by soul singer Al Green. When he made a few Elvis-style pelvic thrusts, the girls in the audience screamed hysterically. Murphy later recalled that, at that moment, "I knew that I was in show biz for the rest of my life."[59]

Fortunately the young entertainer was not alone in his assessment of this situation. It was obvious to almost everyone that this young man had a comic talent that would some-day make him a star. He was

Because of his abilities to make others laugh, Murphy was asked to host a talent show while still in the tenth grade.

often chosen to perform shows at his high school assemblies and one time did a show for each of the six grades of junior high and high school over a period of three days. His newly formed band played at the show, and afterward Murphy did impressions of his teachers and other students. He also worked on comedy routines about the things he knew best—cutting classes, the hardships of gym, and spending after-school hours in detention. By the last day of the performance, students from all grades were filling the auditorium and sitting in the aisles.

By the time he was sixteen Eddie Murphy was headlining in comedy clubs all over Long Island. Until he got his driver's license, Vernon and Lillian would drive him to the gigs. When his mother attended his first performance, however, she was shocked by her son's X-rated routines laced with filthy words. Murphy said he was simply giving the audiences what they wanted, and his step-father believed in him enough to keep driving him to clubs. But Vernon did warn his stepson: "You better become famous or rich, because, boy, you are the laziest kid I've ever seen."[60]

By the time he was seventeen years old, Murphy was earning more than $300 a week, but his grades were suffering because he stayed up late at night rehearsing and writing material. Although he repeatedly told his parents and teachers that he was going to be famous, Murphy failed tenth grade and was told he would have to do it again. This blow to his ego inspired him to attend summer school, night school, and double up on his classes, so in the end he graduated high school only a few months later than his classmates.

After graduation, Vernon forced Murphy to take a "real job" at a shoe store at a local mall. His mother insisted he enroll at Nassau Community College in case his dream of becoming a superstar did not work out. Murphy began classes, majoring in theater, in 1980. But within weeks, at the age of nineteen, he would get that big break that most comedians only dream of.

"Live from New York, It's Saturday Night!"

During the time that Murphy was honing his comedy routines in Long Island clubs, a new phenomenon had taken over late-night Saturday evening television. In 1975 the sketch comedy show *Saturday Night Live (SNL)* had burst onto the scene, running at 11:30 P.M., a time slot previously considered a dead zone by TV networks. By 1979 almost everybody in America was familiar with the show's beloved characters, such as Gilda Radner's Rosanne Rosannadanna, John Belushi's Blues Brothers, and Steve Martin and Dan Aykroyd's "wild and crazy guys." Nightclubs and restaurants began to lose business as millions of people, in an era before the widespread use of VCRs, stayed home on Saturday nights to watch the show.

In the process of becoming America's highest-rated late-night TV show, *Saturday Night Live* made superstars out of most of the original cast. At the end of the 1979 season, the entire cast quit. Hollywood was offering Belushi, Aykroyd, Bill Murray, and others millions of dollars for movie and prime-time television roles.

By 1980 *SNL* was desperately searching for new comedians who could match the outrageous personalities of the departing cast.

Just as they had done in 1975, the producers auditioned groups of unknown comedians. After filling out the cast with a half-dozen white faces, the show set up auditions for the one position open to an African American. When Murphy heard about the auditions, he relentlessly called the show's talent coordinator Neil Levy. Doug Hill and Jeff Weingrad explain Murphy's behavior in *Saturday Night*:

> Murphy . . . had generally been making a nuisance of himself with Levy for several days. He kept calling, sometimes three times a day, insisting he was great, telling sad stories about how desperate he was for a job, and saying all he wanted was a chance to show what he could do.[61]

Murphy was finally given a chance to audition, but the show's new producer, Jean Doumanian, who had auditioned thirty well-known black comedians, hated Murphy's humor. Everyone else at the show, however, laughed hysterically during the young comedian's five subsequent auditions. Putting aside her misgivings about Murphy's youth and lack of experience, Doumanian finally hired the comedian as one of five featured players for $750 a week.

Unfortunately, the 1980–1981 season of *Saturday Night Live* was an unmitigated disaster. After tuning in for four years to the comedic genius of Belushi, Radner, and the rest, Americans were turned off by the revamped show. By February 1981, ratings were extremely low, Doumanian was fired, and a new producer was brought in. By March, the entire new cast was fired except for Murphy and Joe Piscopo. A writers' strike ended the season early, and *SNL* went off the air until September 1981.

"It's the Eddie Murphy Show!"

When *Saturday Night Live* returned in the fall, the producers gave Eddie Murphy free rein. While others in the cast competed for airtime, Murphy starred in more and more of the show's sketches. His salary was raised to $4,500 per show, then to $8,700, and critics wrote glowing reviews, giving Murphy credit for single-handedly saving *Saturday Night Live*. Murphy used his newfound wealth to buy a mansion in Alpine, New Jersey, while moving his parents to a similar house nearby. He also gave tens of thousands of dollars to charities such as the Children's Federation Ethiopian Food Fund.

Money was not Murphy's prime motivation, however. His *SNL* characters generated widespread recognition and instantly became an enduring part of American culture. The comedian hilariously portrayed the Buckwheat character from the 1930s "Little Rascals" comedy films. He mocked children's television host Mr. Rogers with the cutting inner-city "Mr. Robinson's Neighborhood." And he made fun of well-known black stars such as James Brown, Michael Jackson, Stevie Wonder, and others.

By the end of the year, Murphy was the biggest star on television. The comedian had become so famous, in fact, that the producers of *Saturday Night Live* had him host an episode of the show. This was the first time a cast member had been asked to host, and the other players on the show were hurt and angry. When Murphy jokingly finished the show's opening monologue with "Live, from New York, it's the Eddie Murphy show!"[62] several cast members complained bitterly to the producers.

Even though Murphy may have understood his coworkers' resentment, he knew he would not be on the show much longer. By the end of 1982, Hollywood studios were competing to sign the twenty-one-year-old comedian. That year Murphy was offered $1 million plus 10 percent of the gross profits to play the part of slick convict Reggie Hammond in the movie *48 HRS*.

Murphy's easygoing style challenged the ingrained Hollywood assumption that white audiences would not attend movies featur-

Joe Piscopo and Eddie Murphy were the only two cast members asked to return to Saturday Night Live *after the disastrous 1980–1981 season.*

ing tough black men. When reviewing *48 HRS.*, *Newsweek* wrote, "Eddie can tiptoe along the narrow line between anger and laughter in a way that shows everybody how silly we are to imprison ourselves with racial stereotypes."[63] The film eventually made $100 million, earning Murphy nearly $10 million and turning him into the hottest box-office star of the decade.

With his newfound success, Murphy had little desire to return to *Saturday Night Live*. The show's producers, however, claimed that *SNL* would be canceled if Murphy was not on it. This would negatively affect the jobs and lives of the entire staff, many of whom were Murphy's friends. The comedian relented but demanded $300,000 to appear on only ten of the show's twenty episodes. As consolation he offered to tape sketches that could be played on the otherwise live broadcast.

Murphy almost immediately regretted his decision, complaining that the poor writing on the show was damaging his career. In spite of this belief, Murphy won several Emmys for his *SNL* work. When his contract expired in February 1985, Murphy left *Saturday Night Live* without looking back.

Hot New Creative Genius

While Murphy was working at *Saturday Night Live* he had continued to pursue several career paths. In 1982 he released a comedy album titled *Eddie Murphy*, which earned a Grammy award for Best Comedy Album. In 1983 he released *Eddie Murphy: Comedian*, an album that went gold, earning more than $1 million in sales and garnering a second Grammy.

Meanwhile, even before *48 HRS.* debuted, Paramount had signed the comedian to appear with Jamie Lee Curtis and Dan Aykroyd in *Trading Places*, a film about a poor street hustler—played by Murphy—who trades places with a wealthy stockbroker—played by Aykroyd.

While filming the movie, Murphy became known for his disdain of alcohol and drugs. Declaring that he did not want to dull his enjoyment of life with narcotics, he said, "I'm a happy guy. . . . I'm real secure with myself, and I'm not into drugs. . . . My vices are cars and clothes and jewelry. This ring on my finger is *my* cocaine. You can't snort a ring, or else my obituary would be, 'Murphy was found dead with a ring in his nose.'"[64]

When *Trading Places* was released, it became an instant box office smash. *Time* magazine proclaimed Murphy the hottest comic in the business, and the National Association for the Advancement of Colored People (NAACP) awarded him the 1983 Image

While still a member of Saturday Night Live, *Murphy continued to pursue several career paths, including live shows, movies, and comedy albums.*

Award for Best Actor in a Motion Picture. The Hollywood Foreign Press Association nominated him for a Golden Globe.

Paramount, eager to hang on to their hot new creative genius, signed Murphy to a five-picture $15 million contract that would include a percentage of the profits from the films. This contract made show business headlines when it was announced that he would be the first actor ever given a $4 million cash bonus just for signing the contract. Paramount also financed the creation of Eddie Murphy Productions, where the twenty-two-year-old comedian could develop and produce his own projects.

Meanwhile Murphy remained close to his roots, spending most of his time with his parents, brother, and old high school friends. During this period, almost everyone who worked with Murphy commented on his down-to-earth personality as well as his skill as an actor. Veteran actor Ralph Bellamy, who starred opposite Murphy in *Trading Places*, said, "He did these roles as if he'd been in the business all his life. He's like an old-timer. He has professional confidence without intruding on the scene or script. . . . He looked at [costar] Don Ameche and me, not to learn from us, but so as not to take anything away, not to steal a scene. It's rare."[65]

Life in Bubble Hill

Murphy was on a winning streak, and Paramount believed that whatever he touched would turn to gold. His next role, however, demonstrated the fickleness of the viewing public. Murphy accepted an extra $1 million from Paramount to play a small role in *Best Defense*, a Dudley Moore picture that was a major flop.

Murphy's first failure generated gossip that the hot new star was in for a fall. The comedian proved his critics wrong, however, when *Beverly Hills Cop* was released in December 1984.

The script for *Beverly Hills Cop* had been languishing at Paramount for several years when it was offered to Murphy after being turned down by Sylvester Stallone and other hot Hollywood stars. When it was released, however, the film made $64 million in its first three weeks. More than 60 million people saw the movie in theaters, and it eventually pulled in over $235 million, becoming the seventh-highest-grossing picture in history. The success of the film landed Murphy's picture on the cover of *Newsweek*, which proclaimed him "Mr. Box Office." Murphy also received several People's Choice Awards, a Golden Globe, and other accolades.

With unimaginable riches pouring into his bank account, Murphy rewarded himself with a stable of new cars, purchasing a Rolls Royce, a Porsche, a Corvette, a Ferrari, a Jaguar, and others. Needing somewhere to park all these machines, the comedian bought a $3.5 million, twenty-two-room mansion in Englewood Cliffs, New Jersey, with a five-car garage.

Murphy called his new home Bubble Hill. Bubble was a slang expression for party, and Murphy's parties were famous in the mid-1980s. He populated his galas with famous faces such as rock star David Bowie, boxer Sugar Ray Leonard, singers Diana Ross, Stevie Wonder, Sammy Davis Jr., and Garth Brooks, and talk show hosts Arsenio Hall and Dick Cavett.

Visitors to Bubble Hill could not help but marvel at the decor of the nine-thousand-square-foot mansion, as described by Sanello:

> [Each] room in Bubble Hill was decorated in a different style: country, Far Eastern, French Provincial, Victorian, modern. One room was done up entirely in black. His bedroom was stark white, surgical in its pristine decor. There were formal rooms as well as fun rooms. Murphy . . . installed a game room devoted solely to pinball. Other rooms accommodated a pool table and a racquetball court. The inevitable swimming pool was under glass for year-round use. . . . If guests overheated but didn't feel like a dip in the pool, the disco at Bubble Hill featured a rain-

Garth Brooks was just one of the many celebrities to visit Murphy's New Jersey mansion, Bubble Hill.

mist machine to cool off sweaty dancers. A tennis court, with basketball hoops [on each end] provided [rest and recreation] for his underemployed entourage. A rec room looked out on the pool and tennis court. . . . The rec room contained a TV monitor that covered an entire wall, flanked by a bank of stereo gewgaws [showy trinkets]. The recreation area also housed a shrine to Eddie: a life-sized freestanding cardboard cutout of the star wearing his favorite material of the time, leather. Bubble Hill inevitably featured the staple furnishing of the ultrasuccessful in the arts: a screening room. Murphy installed an underground recording studio reached by a tiny elevator that one guest said resembled the transporter room on *Star Trek*.[66]

A Decade of Bad Reviews

While Murphy's friends celebrated his success, the comedian soon began to attract his fair share of critics. The comedian's obscenity-laced stand-up routine, which mocked homosexuals and women —among others—drew scathing attacks when it was broadcast on cable television's HBO and later released on video.

When he tried his hand as a singer on the 1985 album *How Could It Be?* music critics mercilessly panned the "easy listening" dance tunes and mawkish love ballads. Murphy's next movie, *The Golden Child*, about a social worker who must rescue a child reincarnation of Buddha was called a "golden turkey"[67] by *People* magazine even though the movie grossed $100 million. This huge sum of money would have been an outstanding success for anyone else, but it was not considered enough for Eddie Murphy, Hollywood's real golden child.

Murphy sprang back in 1987 with *Beverly Hills Cop 2*, the top-grossing movie of the year, which pulled in $250 million. But the comedian's problems were far from over. Shortly before the debut of *Beverly Hills Cop 2*, Murphy released *Eddie Murphy Raw*, a concert film of his stand-up act at New York's Felt Forum. Murphy had just broken up a three-year relationship with his fiancée Lisa Figueroa, and the movie featured prolonged verbal attacks on women, as well as homosexuals, Asians, Italian Americans, and even African Americans. The critics howled in protest at this politically incorrect humor, but the movie grossed $50 million, becoming the most successful concert film in history.

After *Raw*, however, it seemed the Murphy magic was beginning to wear thin. While 1988's *Coming to America* was successful, 1989's *Harlem Nights*, which Murphy wrote, produced, and directed, was ruthlessly pilloried in the press. Murphy was so hurt and stressed that he began to binge eat, gaining fifteen pounds in a few months.

Murphy's downward spiral continued for almost a decade. *Another 48 HRS.* failed to meet expectations, and *Beverly Hills Cop 3* cost $50 million to make and did not even recoup expenses when released in the United States. As Sanello writes, "The novelty of Eddie making fools out of white cops was ten years old, and fans obviously wanted something new."[68]

The pain of Murphy's bad reviews was softened by the love of his life, Nicole Mitchell, a woman he met at the 1988 NAACP Image Awards in Los Angeles. With stunning good looks, Mitchell had been a fashion model since the age of ten and was earning more than $100,000 a year at the time she met Murphy. The twenty-one-year-old Mitchell moved in with Murphy, who was by now twenty-seven, and the couple had their first child, a girl named Bria, in 1989. The couple would marry in 1992 and have two more children over the course of the next several years.

The Nutty Comeback

In 1996, Murphy finally regained the formula for box-office success with *The Nutty Professor*, a remake of the 1963 Jerry Lewis film. Fans and critics alike were astounded by the multiple roles Murphy played in the film. On the set, the comedian spent hours getting in makeup to portray the family of Professor Sherman Klump. Murphy hilariously played the role of Klump's plump father, doting mother, obscenity-spewing grandmother, and other characters. When the film generated more than $250 million, Murphy was hailed for his remarkable comeback. The comedian also won the Best Actor Award from the National Society of Film Critics.

In 1999, Murphy produced his first TV series, *The PJs*, blending his cutting-edge comedy with "foamation," a type of animated cartoon that uses foam characters. Murphy produced the series and starred as the voice of the lead character, Thurgood Stubbs, the grouchy superintendent of the Hilton-Jacobs housing projects. Though the show had its fans, the controversial series about a group of quirky characters living in an inner-city housing project attracted a chorus of protest from African American critics, who said that the show exploited negative stereotypes about black people for laughs. *The PJs* was dropped from the FOX network after two seasons, and reappeared on the WB's prime-time lineup in the fall of 2000. Later that year, Murphy returned as Professor Sherman Klump and his entire family in *Nutty Professor II.*

Amid the numerous bad reviews of his work, Murphy found happiness after meeting his wife Nicole in 1988.

A comedian for more than half his life before the age of thirty-nine, Eddie Murphy has performed in scores of films and television shows. Although his career has had its ups and downs, he has made hundreds of millions of dollars as an award-winning comedian, actor, singer, writer, director, and producer. While drawing the ire of various minority groups, he has contributed millions to charities. And as a role model for an entire generation of young comedians, Murphy has persistently eschewed drugs and alcohol, remaining a sober family man dedicated to making the world laugh at the foibles common to all.

CHAPTER 5

Jim Carrey

Although Eddie Murphy was one of the top-grossing comedians of the 1980s, his career was eclipsed in the 1990s by Jim Carrey, whose unique brand of goofy physical humor earned him a sky-high salary that set records in Hollywood. Carrey, however, like many other comedy greats, lived through many years of dire poverty as a child.

James Eugene Carrey, the youngest of four children, was born to Kathleen and Percy Carrey in Newmarket, Ontario, a suburb of Toronto, Canada, on January 17, 1962. Jim's father had been a saxophone player of some renown but was forced to give up the life of a jazz musician when he married Kathleen. Instead of leading a big band, Percy took a job at a conservative accounting firm, remaining embittered for years about having to abandon his artistic talents to support his family.

Although the part of his life spent as an accountant may have caused him regrets, Percy was a dedicated and loyal family man. As Carrey told *Esquire* magazine in 1995, "[My father was] the guy who would hand you his shirt in the middle of the desert because you were getting burned—and in the meantime the blisters were swelling up on his own back. He was nice to a fault."[69]

"I Knew What I Wanted"

As a way to rebel against the straight life forced on him, Percy Carrey turned to comedy. At home, he was a madcap jokester widely known among family and friends for his outrageous slapstick humor and practical jokes.

Percy's humor was contagious. The entire Carrey family often engaged in antics such as cherry cheesecake fights at the dinner table. During the Christmas holiday the Carreys were sometimes seen on the front lawn with stockings pulled down over their heads, waving axes at startled passersby.

On the surface the Carreys appeared to be a happy, if nutty, family. There were underlying tensions, however, that caused the Carreys grief. Kathleen was moody, often feigning fatal diseases such as cancer. Her parents were alcoholics who became drunk

Jim Carrey's unique style of physical humor made him one of the most successful entertainers of the 1990s.

and abusive at family gatherings, loudly scolding Percy for not making enough money. To relieve the stress, young Jim learned to imitate his drunken grandparents, cracking up his humiliated father after the older couple had gone home.

As the youngest of four, Jim was often ignored by his brothers and sisters. He quickly realized, however, that making faces, waving his arms around, and hurling his body about the room were great ways to attract attention. As he later recalled,

I used to put on all kinds of shows at home. It was sick, really sick. Every time there was a new person in the house, it was time for me to do the Jim Carrey show. I'd fall down stairs and then go back up and do it in slow motion. Stuff like that. It became nuts after a while.[70]

Like his father, Jim also had a creative, artistic side. Even as a young boy, he wrote songs and poetry, and drew sketches that won awards at school. Nothing, however, could surpass the discovery he made at the age of eight—he could stretch and pull his face into hilarious expressions that no one else could duplicate. The boy spent hours in front of the mirror trying out ridiculous faces and making up bizarre voices to go with them.

When not contorting his face, Jim spent his time watching *The Dick Van Dyke Show* on television, imitating the show's rubber-faced character Rob Petrie. Even at the age of ten, Jim realized that he was destined for a life in show business, sending a short résumé to the producers of *The Carol Burnett Show*. Although he did not receive a response, he was unbowed. He later recalled, "I can't imagine what it's like not to know what you want to do [in life]. . . . I knew what I wanted from the time I was a little kid."[71]

Class Cutup

Carrey hid his outrageous personality when he went to school, becoming shy and withdrawn around strangers. His classmates called him Jimmy-Gene the String Bean because of his rail-thin physique, and he had no friends until third grade, when he realized that if he made faces and told jokes people would like him. When he portrayed the 1930s comedy team the Three Stooges at his second-grade Christmas pageant at Blessed Trinity Catholic School, even the nuns laughed hysterically. Later he broke up the students and teachers with a depiction of an insane Santa Claus.

Unlike comedians such as Bill Cosby and Eddie Murphy, who had high IQs but were mediocre students, Carrey excelled at his schoolwork. He often finished his assignments before his classmates and made faces and jokes as other students tried to complete their work. One frustrated teacher hoped to embarrass the young man by demanding that he stand up in front of the class instead of joking around at his desk. Instead of being scared into silence, Carrey stood up, jammed a handful of mints in his mouth, and, to the delight of his classmates, regurgitated them all over the front row.

In seventh grade one of Carrey's teachers made a deal with him: She would allow him to entertain the class for fifteen minutes at the end of each day if he would not disrupt her lessons the rest of the time. Carrey was thrilled and began to keep track of events at school that he could use in his routines. Occasionally the young comic landed in the principal's office when his hilarious impressions of teachers were a bit too cutting.

A Homeless Dropout

Carrey's happy-go-lucky life was seriously affected when, at the age of thirteen, his father was fired from the accounting firm after thirty-five years of service. Percy, then fifty-one, was considered too old to be hired by another such firm, and he was forced to

In school, Carrey entertained his classmates by making faces, telling jokes, and impersonating various teachers.

take a job as a janitor at the Titan Wheel Factory where steel tire rims were produced for automobiles. Knowing that his father had sacrificed his musical talents only to meet this humiliating end, Carrey vowed to follow his dreams, stating, "It made me realize . . . that life offers no assurances, so you might as well do what you're really passionate about."[72]

Percy's new job paid a fraction of his previous salary so Jim was also obliged to work at Titan Wheel to help support his family. After school, the young man pulled on a janitor's uniform, walked to the factory, and spent eight hours cleaning hallways and bathrooms. Because he was exhausted from work, Carrey's grades fell, his usual As and Bs becoming Cs and Ds. And when his classmates found out he had to work after school, he once again became the target of jokes and insults.

At the age of sixteen, tired, defeated, and friendless, Carrey dropped out of high school. Frustrated and angry with his situation in life, Carrey lashed out, breaking into neighborhood homes, stealing alcohol, and vandalizing local businesses.

The family's downward spiral continued when Percy and Jim, unable to persevere anymore, quit their jobs at the wheel factory. Since they leased their house from Titan Wheel, they were forced to move. The Carreys took up residence in a Volkswagen camper, sleeping in parks in the Toronto area, and occasionally pitching a tent in Jim's oldest sister's yard. Although they were homeless and packed into unheated and cramped quarters, the family regained some of the happiness they had lost after Percy was fired from his accounting job. As Carrey told *Newsweek*, "We didn't have a place to live, but it was like somebody lifted a . . . burden off our shoulders, and we became living, happy, laughing people again, people that had food fights every Sunday."[73]

The end of the 1970s was a time of high unemployment and low economic growth in Canada. Although Percy continued to look for work, nothing was available. The family survived on small donations contributed from friends and family.

From Disaster to Hollywood

Hoping to help his family survive, Carrey decided to pursue his passion for humor at a Toronto comedy club called Yuk Yuks. The nightclub had a weekly "open mike" night when amateurs could get up onstage and try material on an audience made up mostly of other amateur comedians. Percy and Jim labored over a five-minute routine for the young man, and his mother suggested he wear a yellow polyester suit for the big debut.

Jim Carrey was able to exploit the popularity that comedy clubs experienced in the United States and Canada during the 1980s.

Unfortunately Carrey's suit was such a distraction—and his material so bad—that the audience began shouting insults at him before he told his third joke. During the middle of his routine, the club's owner loudly ordered him to leave. As Carrey later recalled,

> I got booed off the stage. . . . I was dressed in a polyester suit that my mom told me would be a good idea, but it didn't go over so well in the hip underground world. . . . I was devastated. . . . That evening was the most awful experience of my life.[74]

Carrey believed in himself, however, and his humiliation was only temporary. Urged on by his father, the comedian continued to hone his act, tirelessly performing at Toronto comedy clubs. Fortunately comedy clubs in Canada and the United States were experiencing unprecedented popularity at this time, and new venues were opening up almost weekly. It was a boom time in the comedy business, and Carrey was there to exploit it.

As Carrey perfected his timing and stage presence, he also worked on more than one hundred impersonations of celebrities such as Frank Sinatra and even Cher. In addition to mimicking voices, Carrey could rearrange his face to look like the person he was imitating. When he returned to Yuk Yuks in 1979, the audience immediately exploded in laughter at his first impression. Before long Carrey was one of the most popular stand-ups in Canada, sometimes earning up to $40,000 for three nights' work. The eighteen-year-old comedian used his newfound wealth to help his family move out of the Volkswagen van and into a rented house.

In 1980, comedian Rodney Dangerfield, who was famous for his "I don't get no respect" routine, saw Carrey's act and hired the young man to open for him on his Canadian tour. After the tour, armed with good reviews, the nineteen-year-old Carrey decided to move to Los Angeles to pursue a career in Hollywood.

Forging a New Path

Carrey experienced culture shock when he moved to a poor section of Los Angeles. He had never seen so many homeless people, prostitutes, and drug dealers. The city was also crowded with thousands of people trying to get a break in show business. Carrey, however, had little trouble establishing himself in Los Angeles comedy clubs. People roared when he made up impersonations on the spot from suggestions shouted out by the audience. By 1982 the comedian was earning a very good salary performing in venues such as the top-rated Comedy Store with future stars such as Robin Williams, Jerry Seinfeld, and David Letterman.

Carrey was in Los Angeles during an era when people were using cocaine in excessive amounts. The young comedian avoided the drug scene, however, preferring to spend his money dating some of Hollywood's most promising actresses. And remembering the lessons learned from his father, Carrey put away extra money in case hard times should suddenly befall him.

Feeling comfortable with his financial situation, Carrey decided to invent a different and unique brand of comedy. Although audiences loved his impersonations, Carrey felt that impressionist comedians had limited career opportunities. His friends, however, thought he had lost his mind. One friend told him, "You're the king of impressions. What are you doing? You're throwing it all away!" Carrey replied that he would never become a superstar by imitating other people. As he explained,

I was putting out something that I didn't want to become known for. I wanted to be myself, to create some things that had never been done before, rather than constantly sitting waiting for the next famous person whom I could impersonate. That held nothing for me. It was a slow realization, but at one point I just said, "never again."[75]

Carrey dropped his act, attended acting classes, and studied videos of comedic actors whom he admired such as Peter Sellers, Jerry Lewis, and Jonathan Winters. Like Lewis, he incorporated physical humor into his act, writhing around on the floor while telling bizarre jokes made up on the spot.

Although maintaining his wild sense of humor, Carrey was suffering in his personal life. He had been supporting his parents for years, but now that he was pursuing a new approach to his career, he sometimes found himself unable to send them money. On one particularly depressing Thanksgiving, the comedian wrote a phony check to himself for $10 million and put it in his wallet as a reminder that one day he would achieve stardom.

Carrey's self-doubts were short-lived. After two years honing his new act, the comedian set out to reestablish himself in the competitive world of Los Angeles comedy clubs. Instead of appearing before audiences with a well-rehearsed act, Carrey jumped on the stage and improvised whatever humor came into his mind at that moment. He combined his old improvisational and physical comedy with bizarre, unpredictable antics. He imitated insane spiders, babbled like a lunatic, or spewed streams of obscenities at hecklers in the audience.

When his act bombed, the comedian would be in tears. After one show, Dangerfield told Carrey that the audience was "lookin' at you like you was from another . . . planet, kid."[76] But when the young comedian's material succeeded, critics, fellow comedians, and audience members alike agreed that there was no one in show business like Jim Carrey.

Trouble at Home

Carrey's new act caught on, and it wasn't long before he was earning up to $200,000 a year. One night in 1982 when the comedian was performing at the Comedy Store, NBC Entertainment president Brandon Tartikoff caught Carrey's act and signed him to star in a new TV series called *The Duck Factory*.

Carrey was cast as an artist who worked as an animator in a cartoon studio. His character interacted with cartoon characters, a concept that was new at that time. Although the show was expected to be a major hit for NBC, it lasted only thirteen weeks. Carrey was miscast as a straight man, and his comedic talents were never utilized on-screen.

Carrey used his first appearances on television as a springboard to obtain small roles in a series of forgettable movies. Although the comedian easily passed auditions by impersonating up to twenty characters and leaving the crew in stitches, directors were unsure what to do with the comedian's formidable talents on the big screen.

Because of his successful act, Rodney Dangerfield asked Carrey to open for him during his 1980 Canadian tour.

Meanwhile, Carrey's parents had come from Canada to live with him, and they were beginning to get on his nerves as they sat around all day watching TV and smoking cigarettes. Carrey commented on the strain this caused in his personal life:

> I resented them for the responsibility of taking care of them since I was 17. I resented them because there had always been a lot of pressure on me to be the star, to save their lives, to buy them the big house with the pillars . . . you know?[77]

To ease the stress, Carrey took the antidepressant medication Prozac, consulted psychics, and read self-help books. Finally his psychotherapist recommended that he send his parents back to Canada, which he did in 1984.

Success on In Living Color

Although Carrey's parents were gone, he did not remain alone for long. The comedian started dating Melissa Wormer, a twenty-six-year-old waitress at the Comedy Store, and the two were married on March 28, 1986. In 1987 the couple had a daughter, Jane.

With his family at the center of his life, Carrey was able to pursue his career in a less stressful manner. He appeared on *The Tonight Show* with Johnny Carson and *The Arsenio Hall Show*. Although he was a hit on the late-night talk show circuit, when he auditioned for *Saturday Night Live* the producers passed him over in favor of Phil Hartman and Dana Carvey.

In 1989 the comedian got a break when he was hired to play an alien in the movie *Earth Girls Are Easy* starring Geena Davis and Jeff Goldblum. Carrey's character was an alien who only spoke gibberish, but his riotous rubber-faced expressions more than made up for his lack of lines. Carrey's costar in *Earth Girls Are Easy* was Damon Wayans, who was very impressed with Carrey's talents.

Damon told Carrey to audition for *In Living Color*, a new TV show being cast by Damon's brother Keenen Ivory Wayans. Carrey was hired for the show but after his experience with *The Duck Factory*, the comedian was not very confident about appearing on another sitcom. Carrey thought that most television shows were horrible, and he did not want to be forced to say lines that he had not written. Wayans reassured the comedian that he would be free to improvise during the show's outrageous skits.

In Living Color was an instant hit after it premiered in April 1990. Carrey cracked up audiences with characters such as Fire Marshal Bill, who set fires rather than put them out. *In Living*

Carrey is seen here with the cast and crew of In Living Color, *the show which catapulted him to stardom.*

Color made Carrey a bona fide star who now had to dodge autograph hounds when he went out on the town.

Hit Movies and Personal Problems

Never content to rest on his past successes, Carrey continued to pursue roles on the big screen. In 1994 he got his biggest break to date when he was signed to star in *Ace Ventura: Pet Detective*, a movie about a detective whose specialty is locating missing pets. The role had been offered to several other comedians, and Carrey himself rejected the role for two years until he was allowed to rewrite the script to suit his own brand of comedy. Carrey was paid $350,000, and spent four months rewriting the script in the wee hours of the morning from midnight to 4:00 A.M. after he had completed taping *In Living Color*. Drawing on his past studies of film comedians, Carrey combined the personalities of Peter Sellers, Robin Williams, and Jerry Lewis to create the unique Ace Ventura.

When *Ace Ventura* was released, most critics hated the film for its low-brow humor. The public, however, loved it, and it was a box-office success.

Flush with success, the producers offered Carrey $7 million to star in a sequel to *Ace Ventura*. Carrey was also offered the same amount to star in *Dumb and Dumber*, a movie about two half-wits who travel across America encountering a number of slapstick mishaps.

As Carrey's career hit the stratosphere, his personal life began to fall apart. Caught up in a whirlwind of television and movie appearances, the comedian was hard-pressed to pay attention to his wife and child. In addition, he was still haunted by a fear of failure and resentment toward his parents. Carrey's wife Melissa often had to sit up with him until 4 or 5 o'clock in the morning counseling him through bouts of severe self-doubt and depression. Eventually, and with much bitterness, the couple divorced.

Although the comedian's personal life was in turmoil, Carrey's next movie, *The Mask,* was an even bigger hit than *Ace Ventura.* To play the role of a mild-mannered bank clerk who turns into a superhero when he puts on a mask, Carrey had to spend up to four hours each day in makeup while technicians applied rubber masks to his face.

When *The Mask* premiered, it made $25 million on its opening weekend, and eventually earned $300 million worldwide. The comedian used his new fortune to purchase a $4 million mansion in the exclusive Brentwood neighborhood of Los Angeles.

Percy and Kathleen barely lived to see their son become a blockbuster Hollywood movie star. Kathleen had died shortly before *Ace Ventura* was made, and Percy died shortly after *The Mask* premiered. At Percy's funeral Carrey took the phony $10 million check he had put in his wallet on that long-ago Thanksgiving and placed it in his father's coffin. He was now a success—he no longer needed the reminder.

Rich and Richer

Alone in the world, Carrey continued with his dizzying career. When *Dumb and Dumber* debuted in December 1994, critics once again savaged the comedian for his doltish character and for the film's liberal use of bathroom humor to get laughs. Bad reviews, however, did not stop the viewing public from making the movie a box-office success. When the film earned more than $100 million, it was Carrey's third hit of the year. Even the comedian himself, who had worked so hard to achieve stardom, could not believe what he had accomplished. He told one interviewer, "It's like Cinderella. Except it's never going to be midnight. . . . Isn't it incredible? There are times when you say, 'What the hell is going on?' "[78]

Carrey's leading lady in *Dumb and Dumber* was Lauren Holly. The couple fell in love on the set and were married in September 1996. Like his other marriage, however, Carrey's neurosis and unpredictability put a strain on the relationship. Carrey and Holly were divorced in ten short months.

Meanwhile, Carrey's success was unstoppable. In 1995 *Ace Ventura* and *The Mask* were both made into Saturday morning cartoons. That same year the comedian was hired to play the villain in *Batman Forever*. When the film opened in June, it made $53.3 million, setting a record for the biggest opening weekend ever.

Elusive Success

Carrey had always believed that success was elusive. And after his fourth blockbuster hit in a row, his doubts were affirmed when the

Carrey's personal problems put a strain on his marriage with Lauren Holly. The couple divorced after ten months.

pet detective sequel, *Ace Ventura: When Nature Calls*, proved to be a box-office bomb. The film was mercilessly panned for lacking humor and originality, and fans stayed away in droves.

After the *Ace Ventura* debacle, Carrey wanted to take his career in a new direction. Rather than starring in a sequence of juvenile comedies, he hoped to be taken more seriously by appearing in dramas. In 1995 he was handed $20 million to appear in the black comedy *The Cable Guy*, about an alienated cable television installer who craves friendship but seeks revenge on those who reject him. His salary made him the highest-paid actor in Hollywood, and Carrey was given creative control over the movie. With so much at stake, the comedian was under major pressure to deliver a huge hit.

When it was released in 1996, *The Cable Guy* made several pointed observations about modern life, television, and personal relationships. Carrey's core base of young fans, however, did not understand or appreciate the film. After grossing $20 million its first weekend, attendance fell off quickly, and the movie was declared a failure. Criticism rolled in from all corners, and an Internet poll showed that 73 percent of those who saw *The Cable Guy* did not like it. Carrey's detractors wrote that the overpaid comedian was washed up.

The Truman Show

At the time *The Cable Guy* premiered, Carrey was already working on his next project, *Liar, Liar*, about a lawyer who cannot tell a lie for twenty-four hours. The film, while billed as a comedy, had a bittersweet, sentimental side that scored big with audiences. The film grossed more than $200 million and restored Carrey's reputation among critics and fans alike.

Still searching for a drama that might win him an Oscar, Carrey starred in *The Truman Show* in 1998. The film, about an unassuming insurance agent, Truman Burbank, whose life had been turned into a televised soap opera without his knowledge, blended science fiction, humor, and drama.

Although Hollywood insiders predicted another flop in the vein of *The Cable Guy*, Carrey's lovable portrayal of Truman Burbank won over audiences. Critics agreed that the story line was solid and interesting. It also foreshadowed the reality-based television programs such as *Survivor* and *Big Brother* that became so popular in 2000.

The Truman Show was a box-office success, and once again, a movie featuring Jim Carrey grossed over $100 million. There was even talk of an Oscar nomination.

As a presenter at the 1999 Academy Awards, Carrey pretends to cry at not being nominated for his performance in The Truman Show.

Carrey's next film, *Man on the Moon*, also blended comedy and drama. In this biography, Carrey portrayed the late comedian Andy Kaufman, who, like Carrey, shocked and entertained audiences with unpredictable improvised stunts. *Man on the Moon* received mixed reviews, but failed to live up to expectations. Carrey's portrayal of Kaufman was so accurate, however, that those who knew the late comedian were startled by the similarities.

"It's Too Important"

Although Carrey's career has had its high and low points, his films earned an astounding $1.5 billion in six short years. And although he earns more than $20 million per picture, he is motivated by his craft and talents, not by money. As he says, "Even if I have $40 million in the bank, if I don't feel that I did a good job that day, I'm a basket case. I'm linked to my work in a probably extremely unhealthy way. It's too important to me."[79]

From living with his family in a Volkswagen van to sailing through the stratosphere of Hollywood's highest peaks, Carrey has maintained his work ethic and his moral compass, if not always his sanity. Although he is now firmly enthroned among the world's immortal comedic geniuses, he still spends his waking hours wracking his brain to think up new ways to make the public laugh. There is little doubt that Jim Carrey will be generating laughter and controversy for as long as he remains in show business.

CHAPTER 6

Chris Rock

Many comedy superstars from Charlie Chaplin to Eddie Murphy started working in show business at a young age. Chris Rock is no exception. By the time he was eighteen he was already appearing regularly at Manhattan comedy clubs.

Rock was only seven years old the first time he heard a Bill Cosby record, and as he was growing up, Rock was exposed to the humor of cutting-edge black comedians such as Richard Pryor and Eddie Murphy. In later years Rock would follow in the footsteps of his early influences, recording best-selling comedy albums and joining the *Saturday Night Live* cast.

Like those influential comedians he learned from, Rock had an inborn understanding of what makes people laugh. And he also knew what wasn't funny. As he told Barry Koltnow of the *Orange County Register*,

> Comedy was the only thing that held my attention when I was a kid. . . . It was also something I seemed to understand. Even though I was only 7, I knew that [the TV show] "Three's Company" was horrible and that they were trying to pass off "Happy Days" as a comedy. I knew those shows weren't funny. None of the sitcoms on television back then were funny. Normally kids laugh at everything, but I wasn't laughing at anything.[80]

Tough Times at School

Chris Rock was born on February 7, 1966, in Georgetown, South Carolina, the oldest of seven children. His father, Julius Rock, was a truck driver who worked three delivery jobs to support his family, and his mother, Rose, was a teacher.

When Chris was six, the family moved to the mean streets of the Bedford-Stuyvesant section of Brooklyn, New York. Bed-Stuy was known for crack dealers and muggings, but the Rock household was located in a peaceful neighborhood where there was little crime. In fact, Chris's upbringing was much like an idyllic family-oriented sitcom, what Rose calls "a black Brady Bunch existence."[81]

Even at a young age, Chris Rock was aware of what made people laugh.

Rock's home life may have been peaceful, but when he began school, he was bused across town to an all-white school in the Bensonhurst neighborhood. Rock was the only black student at the school, and every day he was spit on, beat up, and called "nigger." Instead of learning, the young man spent his school years simply trying to survive. Rock told Christopher John Farley in *Time* magazine,

[Poor] white kids . . . are tough. They're not like your sub-urbanized white kids; they got all this frustration and anger 'cause they're white, for crying out loud, and they're living in America, and they're living as bad as Negroes, for God's sake; so there's no way they're gonna let a scrawny, bused-in black kid from Bed-Stuy have a moment's worth of happiness.[82]

Rock, a small, skinny child, could not fight back, so he tried to turn a bad situation into a tolerable one by making jokes. Unfortunately his humor brought him little relief from the taunts and fists of bullies.

Things did not improve when Rock moved on to high school. Still riding the bus every day, the young man was one of only four black teens in the entire school. Ironically, when Rock returned home, the African American kids in his neighborhood beat him up because they resented him for attending a white high school. Rock recalled those days with Michel Marriott in *Essence*:

Nobody wanted to talk to me . . . I try to forget about all that. . . . Play [sports]? Nothing. Please. The l-a-s-s-s-t guy [picked]. I literally did not have anything, nothing, until I was like famous. . . . I had only been with two women until I got famous. No prom, none of that.[83]

At the age of seventeen Rock dropped out of high school, later earning a general equivalency degree (GED). In need of money to help out his family, the young man went to work as a bus boy at Red Lobster.

Although he was done with school, Rock continued to learn by listening to records from black comedians such as Cosby, Pryor, Dick Gregory, Moms Mabley, and Pigmeat Markham. He also listened to white stand-ups such as Woody Allen and Don Rickles, and classic comedians such as Charlie Chaplin and Groucho Marx. Rock spent hours alone in his room picking up the nuances of timing, delivery, and stage presence. At night, Rock studied the comedians who appeared on *The Tonight Show* with Johnny Carson. He was particularly interested when Cosby was the occasional guest host.

Enter Eddie Murphy

Meanwhile, Rock continued to work at Red Lobster, where, according to Karen S. Schneider, his "streetwise, politically sharp-edged humor cracked up fellow workers."[84]

One night while waiting in line to see Eddie Murphy perform at New York's Radio City Music Hall, the seventeen-year-old Rock noticed a poster announcing an open-mike night at a comedy club called Catch a Rising Star. Rock immediately headed over to the club, lied about his age to get in, and did a five-minute routine that he had been practicing. For the next several years, Rock continued to perform at New York's several comedy clubs, often earning only $5 for a five-minute routine.

Rock got his first big break in 1986 when he was the only African American comic performing at Manhattan's Comic Strip

For several years, Rock performed in New York's comedy clubs, often earning only $5 per routine.

on a night that comedy superstar Eddie Murphy came in. Murphy liked the young comedian immediately, and the two had an instant rapport. Murphy became the young comedian's mentor, hiring Rock for a spot on an HBO stand-up comedy special in 1987, and later for a minor role in *Beverly Hills Cop 2*. In 1988 Rock landed the role of a hip patron of a rib joint in the black detective spoof *I'm Gonna Git You Sucka*.

By the time the movie premiered, however, personal tragedy overshadowed Rock's career. Julius Rock died in 1989 at the relatively young age of fifty-five from complications brought on by a ruptured ulcer. Rock felt terrible, not only for his personal loss but because he had not been making enough to help his family financially while his father was sick. At this low point in his life, Rock almost gave up on his comedy career. When he remembered the words of his father, however, he decided to try with renewed purpose. He told *Jet*,

> My father taught me you have to work for everything and you have to learn to listen to people. And at times you're going to listen to people who you know you are smarter than, but that's what you are going to have to do to get to the next level.[85]

A Featured Player

Rock was able to achieve that next level when he was noticed in *I'm Gonna Git You Sucka* by *Saturday Night Live* producer Lorne Michaels. Michaels liked the comedian's demeanor, and in 1990 the producer hired Rock as a featured player on *SNL*.

It had long been Rock's goal to perform on *SNL*, but he was constantly irritated when people called him "the next Eddie Murphy." As he told Alan Carter in *Essence*, "Eddie and I are cool. He has been very helpful. But everything else, including *Saturday Night Live*, I did on my own. Our comedy is very different."[86]

Unfortunately, Rock's career on *SNL* finally proved to be quite different from his mentor's. While Murphy became a highly paid comedy superstar after his second year on the show, Rock almost faded into the background at *SNL*. He forgot his lines, and his sketches were put on in the last thirty minutes of the ninety-minute show, when many viewers had already tuned out. Talk show host Conan O'Brien, who was a writer for *SNL* during those years, commented on Rock's tenure there: "He was not really in his element. . . . He did some funny stuff on the show, but he was operating at 48% efficiency. He hadn't found his voice."[87]

Rock is pictured with Michael Jordan and the cast of Saturday Night Live. *When he became more concerned about meeting celebrities than learning his lines, Rock's work on* SNL *suffered.*

Part of Rock's problem was that he was blinded by the light of stardom, more concerned with meeting celebrities and having a good time than with working on his lines. The comedian recalled his attitude during his years at *SNL:*

> I never worked as hard as I should have at *SNL.* . . . I was *hanging out.* "You having a party? I'll be there." But you

have sketches to do in the morning. "Sketches smetches," I thought I was cool because I wasn't getting high. But I lived the life of a drug addict, kind of. I wasn't getting sleep, and I wasn't eating, and the focus was all off. [I was] fluffing lines.[88]

"I Was Right Back Where I Started"

Although Rock's voice might have been lost in the crowd at *SNL*, he did have a few memorable characters on the show such as Nat X, a talk show host with a huge Afro hairstyle. And his face was familiar enough to audiences to earn him some better roles on the big screen. In 1991, at the age of twenty-three, Rock played a crack addict turned police informer in a starring role in *New Jack City*.

"New Jack City" is a slang expression for Harlem, the biggest, oldest African American neighborhood in New York City, and the film sparked quite a bit of controversy when it played in big cities across America. Although the movie showed the evils of drug use, it attracted rowdy gangs of teens to theaters. One youth was stabbed in a ticket line where the movie was showing in Boston, and another was shot when exiting a theater in Brooklyn. In Los Angeles, when a theater announced that two evening showings were sold out, about fifteen hundred youths started a riot, looting stores and burning cars. When news of the trouble spread, dozens of theater owners pulled the movie from their schedules. Instead of highlighting the antigang message in the film, the media focused on the gang members who were attending the movie.

Despite the controversy, the critics gave Rock great reviews for his role in the film. Things were going badly, however, at *SNL*. The quality of Rock's sketches was uneven, and he was messing up his lines. Finally in 1993, Michaels let Rock out of his five-year contract two years early.

Even before Rock quit *SNL*, he had been offered a featured role on the African American sketch comedy show *In Living Color*, where he would be given more artistic freedom. Adding to his streak of bad luck, however, *In Living Color* had been foundering for some time, and the show went off the air after only eight episodes with Rock.

His television ventures at a standstill, Rock released *Born Suspect*, a CD of his stand-up routine. Later he wrote and costarred in *CB4*, a film parody of rap music and the gangster lifestyle. Although these projects garnered great reviews, the CD was not a hot seller and *CB4* did poorly at the box office. Rock was out of work, and as he said,

[When] you're in show business, when you ain't working, you're unemployed. . . . I was right back where I started—playing little clubs, you know. . . . I had accomplished nothing, really. I'd done everything but nothing well. I was famous, but everybody's famous. . . . No one said they liked my work. They just said, "Hey, I saw you on that show."[89]

To make matters worse, his delivery and timing had grown stale. When he did his first live show at the end of his *SNL* run, he was badly upstaged by the warm-up act, Martin Lawrence. Meanwhile, Rock's black audience had abandoned him during his *SNL* years; he could not get bookings at African American colleges or nightclubs. And the material he did about housing projects, single mothers, and tough Brooklyn neighborhoods did not play well to white audiences.

Politically Incorrect Comedy

Like a major-league player sent back to the minor leagues, Rock was forced to return to tiny comedy clubs, where he occasionally performed to empty rooms. With his past successes played out, Rock felt he had no choice but to follow his father's advice and work as hard as ever. He quit going to parties, began getting up early in the morning, and started eating properly. He honed his material and practiced like he had in the early days. And Rock wrote a slew of new jokes, becoming what he called a hip-hop comedian, with rapid-fire routines and in-your-face honesty reminiscent of hip-hop music.

Rock gradually regained his black audience and earned a reputation for uttering hard truths about black-on-black crime and black-white race relations. In *Rock This!*, a book of his stand-up comedy routines, the comedian expounds on these topics:

I once took a black history class. I figured since I'm black I already knew everything. I figured I'd pass just by showing up.

Failed it.

Isn't that sad, a black man failing black history? But I didn't know anything about Africa. When you go to white schools you learn about Europe . . . but you don't learn that much about Africa. The only thing I know about Africa is that it's far, far away. A 35-hour [airplane] flight. Imagine the boat ride. The boat ride's so long there's still slaves on their way here.

All I learned in school about being black was Martin Luther King. That's all they ever teach. Martin Luther King. He was the answer to everything.

TEACHER: What's the capital of Zaire?

ME: Martin Luther King.

TEACHER: Tell us the name of the woman who would not give up her seat on the bus.

After a period of less-than-stellar performances, Rock gradually regained black audiences and in the process, earned a reputation for uttering harsh truths about black life.

ME: Oh, that's hard. Are ya sure it was a woman? Okay, I got it: Mar*tina* Luther King.

You know what's sad? Martin Luther King stood for non-violence. Now that he's dead he stands for a holiday and a street. Martin Luther King Boulevard. No matter where you are in America, you'll find one. And you can be certain that if you're on Martin Luther King Boulevard, there's some violence going down. It isn't the safest place to be. You can't call anybody and say you're lost on MLK.[90]

In May 1996, Rock taped his stand-up act at the Takoma Theater in Washington, D.C., for an HBO special called *Bring on the Pain*. The show was replayed frequently on HBO, and the formerly unemployed comic suddenly became a comedy superstar. Offers poured in for commercial endorsements, movie roles, and television specials. His routines also generated their share of controversy, especially in the African American community. As Kevin L. Carter wrote,

[In] "Bring on the Pain," [Rock] is . . . serious and brutally frank in his assessments of black shortcomings. He rails against people he considers "niggers" rather than "black people," and speaks very harshly against the high crime rate in black communities. That, in a nutshell, is the way he differentiates between those African Americans who are law-abiding and hard-working and those who aren't.

And people who act in what the comic considers a negative manner—such as unwed welfare mothers having children by several different men or those who blame "the white man" or "the media" for their troubles—are often targets of Rock's barbs. . . .

Rock is also very critical of blacks who disparage others of their race for aspiring to do well in school, to speak standard English, and to live a middle-class existence. But he is also scathingly disparaging of whites whom he considers racists.[91]

Riding High

Buoyed by the success of *Bring on the Pain*, which won two Emmy awards in 1996, Rock made some changes in his personal life. Hoping for stability in the fast-paced world of entertainment, Rock married his girlfriend Malaak Compton, a public relations executive for a nonprofit organization. Rock met Compton at an awards show in 1992. There was an instant and mutual attraction, but it took several years for the couple to get together. Marriage seemed to suit Rock, as he commented in *Jet:*

> [Marriage] calms you down. It definitely calms you down. You have a home. It provides some stability. I am a comedian; do you know how unstable that is? She's really centered me. She's really calmed me down and centered my life.[92]

With a secure home life, Rock continued to take advantage of his position as "hot young comedian," working in a series of ads aimed at the youth market. He provided the screeching voice of a puppet named Little Penny Hardaway in Nike sneaker commercials and appeared as a spokesman for MCI's 1-800-COLLECT telephone service.

Rock also appeared on the irreverent current events comedy show *Politically Incorrect*, covering the Republican presidential convention in San Diego. There he made pithy comments such as "There's enough crackers here to sop up the Atlantic Ocean."[93]

With the success of his comedy special, HBO offered Rock a weekly thirty-minute series called *The Chris Rock Show*, in which the comedian made succinct comments about the foibles of celebrities and travelled around the New York City area highlighting humor from everyday people in the streets. Rock worked hard on the show, spending up to ten hours a day writing jokes and perfecting their delivery.

Rock on a Roll

Chris Rock was definitely on a roll. He hosted the MTV Music Video Awards in 1997 (and would host again in 1999). When he released his book *Rock This!* in September 1997, it became an instant best-seller, with his fans snapping up 185,000 copies in four months. The book's sales were fueled by an hour-long appearance on *The Oprah Winfrey Show*.

In early 1998, the comedian was featured in a segment on *60 Minutes*, and later that year Rock starred with Mel Gibson and Danny Glover in *Lethal Weapon 4*. Some critics claimed that Rock's on-screen humor stole the show from the well-established superstar Gibson.

Despite his mainstream success, Rock remained a center of controversy. In August 1998, the comedian's appearance was cut from the West Coast broadcast of the TV show *Today* when he said he was going to "whup [special prosecutor] Kenneth Starr's ass"[94] for promoting the impeachment of President Bill Clinton.

No stranger to political firestorms, Rock generated religious controversy when he appeared in the independent film *Dogma* as the fictional thirteenth apostle who was written out of history because

Hoping to gain some stability in his life, Rock married his girlfriend Malaak Compton.

Rock's candor and honesty have made him a target of political and religious controversy, but they have also propelled him to newfound success.

he dared to reveal that Jesus was actually black. Religious groups protested the release of the irreverent comedy, but Rock told his critics,

> Everything should be satirized and skewered. Nothing is above jokes and that includes religion. No, make that especially religion because religion takes itself much too seriously. . . . I don't want to go to heaven if it ain't funny. I don't see heaven as a bunch of comedy clubs, but I do see it as a lot of people laughing.[95]

Dogma did not do well at the theaters, at least partly because of the controversy, but the undaunted comedian continued to walk the tightrope between humor and controversy. In 2000, he played a ruthless hit man in the film *Nurse Betty*, which juggled slapstick comedy with gallows humor. Meanwhile, *The Chris Rock Show* was nominated for six Emmys in 2000.

The Rock Philosophy

For all his spewing of four-letter words and his notoriously hot-button approach to humor, Rock remains a religious man devoted to his family. He reads the Bible often, finding strength in the Proverbs, and he donates a portion of his wealth to charity. Rock has also used his riches to support his mother and family. His wife doesn't have to work, and although the marriage was rocky for several years, the couple remains dedicated to each other.

Chris Rock spent sixteen years becoming an "overnight sensation." Growing up, he faced years of prejudice and hardship in school, and was unemployed several times during his long career after stunning opportunities turned to ashes. When his father died, he almost gave up comedy forever.

It was the words of his father, however, that echoed in Rock's head during his lowest moments, reminding him to work hard and listen to other people. Those words of wisdom buoyed Rock's spirits and helped him rise to the top in a tough, competitive business. As he told *Jet*,

> You just live a life. . . . You just keep quiet and observe, try to be around normal people. . . . The barber shop is a great place. I have a crazy life. My family is pretty normal. I have my brothers, sister and my mother; you just draw from all the people around you. I read about four or five newspapers a day and every magazine I can get my hands on to try to get a sense of what's going on in the country.[96]

Chris Rock's humor may not be for everyone, but his candor and honesty are valued by his fans, who look forward to a dose of the truth in a sometimes superficial world.

Notes

Introduction: Laughing to Keep from Crying

1. Quoted in Gabriel Robins, "Good Quotations from Famous People," July 7, 2000. www.cs.virginia.edu/~robins/quotes.html.

Chapter 1: Charlie Chaplin

2. Charles Chaplin, *Charles Chaplin: My Autobiography*. New York: Simon & Schuster, 1964, p. 14.

3. Chaplin, *My Autobiography*, p. 18.

4. Chaplin, *My Autobiography*, p. 20.

5. Chaplin, *My Autobiography*, p. 21.

6. Peter Guttmacher, *Legendary Comedies*. New York: Metro Books, 1996, p. 18.

7. Chaplin, *My Autobiography*, p. 71.

8. Chaplin, *My Autobiography*, p. 89.

9. Chaplin, *My Autobiography*, p. 101.

10. Quoted in Kenneth S. Lynn, *Charlie Chaplin and His Times*. New York: Simon & Schuster, 1997, p. 89.

11. Quoted in Chaplin, *My Autobiography*, p. 141.

12. Guttmacher, *Legendary Comedies*, p. 18.

13. Guttmacher, *Legendary Comedies*, p. 18.

14. Quoted in Robyn Karney and Robin Cross, *The Life and Times of Charlie Chaplin*. New York: Smithmark, 1992, p. 73.

15. Karney and Cross, *The Life and Times of Charlie Chaplin*, p. 73.

16. Karney and Cross, *The Life and Times of Charlie Chaplin*, p. 82.

17. Guttmacher, *Legendary Comedies*, p. 20.

18. Chaplin, *My Autobiography*, p. 320.

19. Quoted in Karney and Cross, *The Life and Times of Charlie Chaplin*, p. 106.

20. Quoted in Arthur Diamond, *The Importance of Charlie Chaplin*. San Diego: Lucent Books, 1995, p. 86.

21. Quoted in Karney and Cross, *The Life and Times of Charlie Chaplin*, p. 115.

Chapter 2: Groucho Marx

22. Groucho Marx, *The Groucho Phile*. Indianapolis: Bobbs-Merrill, 1976, p. 11.

23. Marx, *The Groucho Phile*, p. 15.

24. Marx, *The Groucho Phile*, p. 18.

25. Guttmacher, *Legendary Comedies*, pp. 37–38.

26. Marx, *The Groucho Phile*, p. 40.

27. Quoted in Marx, *The Groucho Phile*, p. 48.

28. Marx, *The Groucho Phile*, p. 41.

29. Arthur Marx, *My Life with Groucho*. London: Robson Books, 1988, pp. 59–60.

30. Marx, *My Life with Groucho*, p. 76.

31. Quoted in Marx, *My Life with Groucho*, p. 90.

32. Quoted in Marx, *My Life with Groucho*, p. 90.

33. Marx, *My Life with Groucho*, p. 89.

34. Quoted in Marx, *My Life with Groucho*, p. 97.

35. Marx, *The Groucho Phile*, p. 106.

36. Guttmacher, *Legendary Comedies*, p. 38.

37. Quoted in Guttmacher, *Legendary Comedies*, p. 37.

38. Marx, *The Groucho Phile*, p. 207.

39. Marx, *The Groucho Phile*, p. 234.

40. Marx, *The Groucho Phile*, p. 248.

41. Marx, *My Life with Groucho*, p. 286.

Chapter 3: Bill Cosby

42. Quoted in Bill Adler, *The Cosby Wit: His Life and Humor*. New York: Carroll & Graf, 1986, p. 13.

43. Quoted in Ronald L. Smith, *Cosby*. New York: St. Martin's Press, 1986, pp. 9–10.

44. Quoted in Smith, *Cosby*, p. 10.

45. Smith, *Cosby*, p. 18.

46. Quoted in Adler, *The Cosby Wit*, p. 15.

47. Smith, *Cosby*, p. 29.

48. Smith, *Cosby*, p. 30.

49. Smith, *Cosby*, pp. 33–34.

50. Adler, *The Cosby Wit*, p. 22.

51. Quoted in Smith, *Cosby*, p. 68.

52. Quoted in Smith, *Cosby*, p. 151.

53. Smith, *Cosby*, p. 179.

54. Quoted in Smith, *Cosby*, p. 183.

55. "Bill Cosby," Kennedy Center Honors, 1998. http://kennedy-center.org/honors/history/honoree/cosby.html.

Chapter 4: Eddie Murphy

56. Quoted in Frank Sanello, *Eddie Murphy*. New York: Birch Lane Press, 1997, p. 4.

57. Quoted in Sanello, *Eddie Murphy*, pp. 4, 5.

58. Sanello, *Eddie Murphy*, p. 10.

59. Quoted in Sanello, *Eddie Murphy*, p. 19.

60. Quoted in Sanello, *Eddie Murphy*, p. 20.

61. Doug Hill and Jeff Weingrad, *Saturday Night*. New York: Beech Tree Books, 1986, p. 391.

62. Quoted in Hill and Weingrad, *Saturday Night*, p. 467.

63. Quoted in Sanello, *Eddie Murphy*, pp. 41–42.

64. Quoted in Sanello, *Eddie Murphy*, p. 66.

65. Quoted in Marianne Ruuth, *Eddie*. Los Angeles: Holloway House, 1985, p. 111.

66. Sanello, *Eddie Murphy*, pp. 103–104.

67. Quoted in Sanello, *Eddie Murphy*, p. 113.

68. Sanello, *Eddie Murphy*, p. 242.

Chapter 5: Jim Carrey

69. Quoted in Martha Sherrill, "Renaissance Man," *Esquire*, December 1995, p. 103.

70. Quoted in Laurie Lanzen Harris, ed., *Biography Today*. Detroit: Omnigraphics, 1998, p. 36.

71. Quoted in Roy Trakin, *Jim Carrey Unmasked!* New York: St. Martin's Paperbacks, 1995, p. 18.

72. Quoted in Trakin, *Jim Carrey Unmasked!* p. 19.

73. Quoted in Jeff Giles, "Funny Face," *Newsweek*, June 26, 1995, p. 51.

74. Quoted in Trakin, *Jim Carrey Unmasked!* p. 23.

75. Quoted in Harris, *Biography Today*, p. 39.

76. Quoted in Trakin, *Jim Carrey Unmasked!* p. 60.

77. Quoted in Harris, *Biography Today*, p. 39.

78. Quoted in Scott and Barbara Siegel, eds., *The Jim Carrey Scrapbook*. New York: Citadel Press, 1995, p. 84.

79. Quoted in Harris, *Biography Today*, p. 43.

Chapter 6: Chris Rock

80. Quoted in Barry Koltnow, "Chris Rock's Comedy Is Pointed, but He Won't Agree He's a Social Commentator," *Orange County Register*, April 22, 1997. http://web7.infotrac.galegroup.com/itw/infomark/513/758/72709790w3/purl=rc1_GRCM_0_CJ19333886&dyn=4!xrn_1_0_CJ19333886?sw_aep=sddp_informe.

81. Quoted in Karen S. Schneider, "High-Flying *Saturday Night Live* Comic Chris Rock Soars in His *New Jack City* Film Role," *People Weekly*, March 25, 1991, p. 75.

82. Quoted in Christopher John Farley, "Rock Star," *Time*, July 20, 1998, p. 56.

83. Quoted in Michel Marriott, "Rock on a Roll," *Essence*, November 1998, p. 116.

84. Schneider, "High-Flying *Saturday Night Live* Comic Chris Rock," p. 76.

85. Quoted in *Jet*, "Chris Rock Talks About His Comedy, New Wife, and Fame," October 20, 1997, p. 32.

86. Quoted in Alan Carter, "Chris Rock," *Essence*, April 1991, p. 31.

87. Quoted in Farley, "Rock Star," p. 56.

88. Quoted in Fred Schruers, "Chris Rock," *Rolling Stone*, October 2, 1997, p. 64.

89. Quoted in Schruers, "Chris Rock," p. 64.

90. Chris Rock, *Rock This!* New York: Chris Rock Enterprises, 1997, pp. 26–27.

91. Kevin L. Carter, "His Politically Incorrect Comedy Has Made Chris Rock a Hot Property," *Philadelphia Inquirer*, August 15, 1996, p. 815.

92. Quoted in *Jet*, "Chris Rock Talks About His Comedy, New Wife, and Fame," p. 32.

93. Quoted in Carter, "His Politically Incorrect Comedy Has Made Chris Rock a Hot Property," p. 815.

94. Quoted in *People Weekly*, "Chris Rock: His Edgy Comic Candor Provoked an Avalanche of Laughs," December 28, 1998, p. 62.

95. Quoted in JAM, "Chris Rock," November 13, 1999. www.canoe.ca/JamMoviesArtistsR/rock_chris.html.

96. Quoted in *Jet*, "Chris Rock Talks About His Comedy, New Wife, and Fame," p. 32.

FOR FURTHER READING

Bruce W. Concord, *Bill Cosby*. New York: Chelsea House, 1993. A biography about the life and comedy of Bill Cosby that is part of the "Junior World Biography" series for elementary and middle school readers.

Bill Cosby, *Childhood*. New York: G. P. Putnam's Sons, 1991. A humorous best-selling book about the trials and tribulations of childhood by one of America's most beloved comedians.

Arthur Diamond, *The Importance of Charlie Chaplin*. San Diego: Lucent Books, 1995. A fascinating and informative biography of Charlie Chaplin focusing on his life and his films.

Peter Guttmacher, *Legendary Comedies*. New York: Metro Books, 1996. Filled with photographs, witty text, humorous quotes, and trivia concerning the legendary comedy movies of the past eighty years, this book covers the films of Charlie Chaplin, Groucho Marx, Jim Carrey, and others.

Robyn Karney and Robin Cross, *The Life and Times of Charlie Chaplin*. New York: Smithmark, 1992. A large colorful book that traces Charlie Chaplin's rise to stardom, with detailed descriptions of his many films.

Groucho Marx, *The Groucho Phile*. Indianapolis: Bobbs-Merrill, 1976. A book with nearly seven hundred photographs of Groucho and the Marx Brothers, from early childhood to vaudeville, Broadway, Hollywood, and beyond. Each photograph is accompanied by a humorous description by Groucho explaining the time, place, and behind-the-scenes information.

Michael A. Schuman, *Bill Cosby: Actor and Comedian*. Springfield, NJ: Enslow, 1995. A biography of Bill Cosby by a widely published author who conducted interviews with people close to Cosby to produce an insightful and well-written book.

Deborah A. Wilburn, *Eddie Murphy*. New York: Chelsea House, 1993. A biography of Eddie Murphy, part of the "Black Americans of Achievement" series, that includes details about his life, comedy, and film history.

John F. Wukovits, *Jim Carrey*. San Diego: Lucent Books, 1999. A well-researched, interesting, and detailed biography of Jim Carrey from his impoverished childhood in Canada to his stardom in Hollywood.

WORKS CONSULTED

Books

Bill Adler, *The Cosby Wit: His Life and Humor*. New York: Carroll & Graf, 1986. The story of Bill Cosby's life, career, and family, and a behind-the-scenes look at the humor of one of America's most beloved comedians.

Charles Chaplin, *Charles Chaplin: My Autobiography*. New York: Simon & Schuster, 1964. The autobiography from the comedy great himself told with sensitivity and humorous charm.

Laurie Lanzen Harris, ed., *Biography Today*. Detroit: Omnigraphics, 1998. A book with the biographies of several notable people, including Jim Carrey.

Doug Hill and Jeff Weingrad, *Saturday Night*. New York: Beech Tree Books, 1986. A backstage look at the TV show *Saturday Night Live*, with all the laughter, tears, genius, egos, and occasional tragedy.

Kenneth S. Lynn, *Charlie Chaplin and His Times*. New York: Simon & Schuster, 1997. A modern biography of Chaplin that explores the parties, prostitutes, and controversial politics of one of the world's most beloved comedians.

Arthur Marx, *My Life with Groucho*. London: Robson Books, 1988. A behind-the-scenes book about Groucho Marx that portrays him as a loving family man and a quirky nonconformist. The book is written by his son, who is also the author of half a dozen books and several plays.

Chris Rock, *Rock This!* New York: Chris Rock Enterprises, 1997. A collection of Rock's best jokes from his hilarious *Bring on the Pain* HBO special.

Marianne Ruuth, *Eddie*. Los Angeles: Holloway House, 1985. A paperback biography of Eddie Murphy written at the height of his stardom after *Beverly Hills Cop*, with twenty-four pages of photographs and the actor's horoscope.

Frank Sanello, *Eddie Murphy*. New York: Birch Lane Press, 1997. The life and times of Eddie Murphy written by a former film critic from the *Los Angeles Times*.

Scott and Barbara Siegel, eds., *The Jim Carrey Scrapbook*. New York: Citadel Press, 1995. A book of photos and information about Jim Carrey's life and career arranged in a scrapbook format.

Ronald L. Smith, *Cosby*. New York: St. Martin's Press, 1986. A biography of Bill Cosby culled from interviews with friends, family, and colleagues.

Roy Trakin, *Jim Carrey Unmasked!* New York: St. Martin's Paperbacks, 1995. A biography of Jim Carrey that explores the comedian's childhood, his life as a struggling stand-up, and his skyrocket to fame.

Periodicals

Alan Carter, "Chris Rock," *Essence*, April 1991. An insightful article about Chris Rock published during the comedian's debut season on *Saturday Night Live*.

Kevin L. Carter, "His Politically Incorrect Comedy Has Made Chris Rock a Hot Property," *Philadelphia Inquirer*, August 15, 1996. A newspaper article on how Chris Rock's outrageous comedy sometimes offends those who follow politically correct standards.

Christopher John Farley, "Rock Star," *Time*, July 20, 1998. An article about the life of Chris Rock written when the comedian was considered one of Hollywood's hottest actors, costarring in *Lethal Weapon 4*.

Jeff Giles, "Funny Face," *Newsweek*, June 26, 1995. An article about Jim Carrey written when the comedian was beginning to emerge as one of Hollywood's top stars.

Jet, "Chris Rock Talks About His Comedy, New Wife, and Fame," October 20, 1997. An article featuring Chris Rock's life and career.

Michel Marriott, "Rock on a Roll," *Essence*, November 1998. An article about the life and times of Chris Rock, who comments on his childhood, his movie roles, and his award-winning HBO special.

People Weekly, "Chris Rock: His Edgy Comic Candor Provoked an Avalanche of Laughs," December 28, 1998. A brief article about Chris Rock's fame and his projects in 1998.

Karen S. Schneider, "High-Flying *Saturday Night Live* Comic Chris Rock Soars in His *New Jack City* Film Role," *People Weekly*, March 25, 1991. An article written when Chris Rock's career was taking off after his first major film appearance.

Fred Schruers, "Chris Rock," *Rolling Stone*, October 2, 1997. A biographical article about Chris Rock, his old neighborhood, and his daily life at home.

Martha Sherrill, "Renaissance Man," *Esquire*, December 1995. A detailed article about Jim Carrey, his life, and his movie roles.

Websites

"Bill Cosby," Kennedy Center Honors, 1998. http://kennedy-center.org/honors/history/honoree/cosby.html. A brief biography of Bill Cosby's career and why he was honored by the respected Kennedy Center for the Performing Arts.

JAM, "Chris Rock," November 13, 1999. www.canoe.ca/JamMovies ArtistsR/rock_chris.html. A Canadian website that features articles about music, movies, video, television, books, and other media.

Barry Koltnow, "Chris Rock's Comedy Is Pointed, but He Won't Agree He's a Social Commentator," *Orange County Register*, April 22, 1997. http://web7.infotrac.galegroup.com/itw/infomark/513/758/72709790w3/purl=rc1_GRCM_0_CJ19333886&dyn=4!xrn_1_0_CJ19333886?sw_aep=sddp_informe. An article about the life and humor of Chris Rock.

Gabriel Robins, "Good Quotations from Famous People," July 7, 2000. www.cs.virginia.edu/~robins/quotes.html. Famous pithy quotes from Charles Dickens, Voltaire, Groucho Marx, Bill Gates, and other intellectuals.

PICTURE CREDITS

ABOUT THE AUTHOR

Stuart A. Kallen is the author of more than 150 nonfiction books for children and young adults. He has written young adult books on topics ranging from the theory of relativity to the history of rock 'n' roll. In addition, Mr. Kallen is the author of award-winning children's videos and television scripts. In his spare time, Mr. Kallen is a singer/songwriter/guitarist in San Diego, California.